THE 'HIDDEN' DEBT

FINANCIAL AND MONETARY POLICY STUDIES

Volume 19

The titles published in this series are listed at the end of this volume.

The 'Hidden' Debt

by

ILDE RIZZO

Università di Catania
Facoltà di Economia e Commercio
Istituto di Finanza Pubblica
Corso Italia 55
95129 Catania
Italia

KLUWER ACADEMIC PUBLISHERS

DORDRECHT / BOSTON / LONDON

Library of Congress Cataloging-in-Publication Data

Rizzo, Ilde.
    The "hidden" debt / Ilde Rizzo.
        p.   cm. -- (Financial and monetary policy studies ; 19)
    Includes bibliographical references.
    ISBN 0-7923-0610-4
    1. Old age pensions--Great Britain--Finance. 2. Debts, Public-
-Great Britain. 3. Social choice--Great Britain.   I. Title.
II. Series.
HD7105.35.G7R59   1990
336.3'4'0941--dc20

89-26728

ISBN 0-7923-0610-4

Published by Kluwer Academic Publishers,
P.O. Box 17, 3300 AA Dordrecht, The Netherlands.

Kluwer Academic Publishers incorporates
the publishing programmes of
D. Reidel, Martinus Nijhoff, Dr W. Junk and MTP Press.

Sold and distributed in the U.S.A. and Canada
by Kluwer Academic Publishers,
101 Philip Drive, Norwell, MA 02061, U.S.A.

In all other countries, sold and distributed
by Kluwer Academic Publishers,
P.O. Box 322, 3300 AH Dordrecht, The Netherlands.

Printed on acid-free paper

Table of contents

Foreword

Some years ago, when Principal and Professor of Economics at the infant University of Buckingham, Britain's only independent university, I was intrigued to receive an application, supported by strong recommendations from a Signora Ilde Rizzo, who wished to take some courses in public finance. As she was already an Assistant at the University of Catania, noted for its expertise in the economics of public finance, my colleagues and I brushed aside her modest request to attend undergraduate courses and enrolled her in our new graduate course. We also hoped that she might, in time, be able to gain experience in teaching and writing in English. Dr. Rizzo exceeded our highest expectations. She presented the first D.Phil thesis ever at Buckingham and defended it with consummate success. This work is a revised and extended version of her thesis, and it is a pleasure to congratulate Dr. Rizzo on its appearance, and also her publisher for recognizing its quality. It will come as no surprise to the reader that Dr. Rizzo has already published extensively in Italian and also in English, but this is her first book in the latter language.

I am glad to think that Dr. Rizzo's thesis arose out of our mutual interest in the question as to whether debt financing offered governments a major opportunity for maintaining the growth of public spending. This led us to consider the dimensions of public debt and cogitation over how to treat unfunded future obligations of government, notably contracts to pay state retirement pensions. We demonstrated the modifications that this 'hidden' debt would introduce into the formulation of the Buchanan/Wagner hypothesis and the associated attempts to test that hypothesis in a joint article in *Public Finance* 1987. Dr. Rizzo was quick to see that a more thorough investigation of the difference between funded and unfunded debt could be made, while still employing a public choice framework. Clearly, there are important differences to be highlighted between the contracts made between the citizen and the state in respect of funded and unfunded debt. Furthermore, the prospect of the growth in the relative importance of state pensions as a result of demographic changes offers good practical reasons why one should be clear about the way in which the drawing up of a contract between present generations regarding state pension rights would affect future generations of voters/taxpayers who would have no initial 'say' in the specification of such a contract. If the welfare of future generations is recognized as a public good, how far can this and will this be reflected in the claims made on future resources exercised through a state pension system? How does one measure the 'burden', if that is the right word, of unfunded debt on future generations?

Dr. Rizzo's contribution is not designed to produce specific answers to policy questions. That would in any case require her to go beyond the dimensions of economic analysis. What she has done is more fundamental which is to identify the proper analytical framework for the study of such questions. The reader will soon discover for himself or herself that Dr. Rizzo writes with an interest, enthusiasm and professionalism which compels attention. At the same time while her approach may owe something to her sojourn abroad, she remains true to her intellectual birthplace. The transpiration of Italian writing, much of it shamefully neglected outside its country of origin, is the binding force in her exposition, which is entirely as it should be.

November 1989   Alan T. Peacock

Acknowledgements

This study develops out of a D.Phil thesis carried out at the University of Buckingham under the supervision of Martin Ricketts to whom I am grateful for support, help and precious suggestions, without which it would have been most difficult to pursue my research.

I am especially indebted to Alan T. Peacock, for his invaluable suggestions, advice and encouragement; without his help this book might never have reached the printer. I am grateful also to Emilio Giardina who has provided support, encouragement and helpful insights for the development of the research. My thanks are also due to Peter Jackson and Zaphirius Tzannatos for helpful comments on some parts of my work and to Keith Shaw for his advice and encouragement. It goes without saying that any errors that remain are my responsibility alone.

My thanks are also due to the University of Buckingham for the financial support I have received to undertake my research and to Linda Waterman for the careful assistance given in the editing of this work.

1. Introduction

1.1 The study is concerned with the analysis of the pension debt issue. Such an issue constitutes a matter of increasing interest in the professional literature because of its relevant allocational, distributional and macroeconomic implications. Not all these questions will be dealt with in this study. More precisely, macroeconomic effects will not be discussed here and attention will be paid only to some specific allocational and distributional aspects, which will be examined below.

The analysis is mainly positive: we do not try to answer any questions regarding the desirability of a social security system but only to investigate its likely distributional and allocational effects, under some individual behavioural assumptions which will be outlined below in more detail.

The primary issue studied is the way in which the phenomenon of ageing affects the functioning of a PAYG (Pay As You Go) pension system, from the specific point of view of its collective decision-making outcome. Our aim is to formulate a broad theoretical framework to determine whether such demographic changes do, indeed, lead to the continuous expansion of the PAYG system, through the functioning of the collective decision-making process, as is usually claimed in the literature. This study tries to suggest that such a conventional conclusion does not necessarily hold. To support such a thesis, the constraints imposed on individual choices should be stressed. Rational self-interest, in fact, is likely to induce individuals not to place too great a burden on the system. The fulfilment of unfunded obligation is uncertain, because of the lack of temporal coincidence between benefits and costs; if its burden on the working generation becomes too heavy, the fulfilment itself might be discouraged.

Following the same line of reasoning, the only normative insight stemming from this study is the suggestion that the uncertainty of pension obligation can be reduced if a suitable system of fulfilment is devised, the main purpose being the fair sharing of the "demographic risk" underlying such an obligation. To serve this purpose a form of fulfilment is suggested.

This study is concerned only with a stylised PAYG system and no attempt is made to take into account alternative social security arrangements. Indeed, real systems differ from such an ideal model. Each presents specific features; therefore, it is difficult to devise a more realistic model, suitably representing the various different real systems. Thus, in order to make the analysis as general as possible it seems better to make reference to the original ideal PAYG model.

Having defined in very broad terms the main scope of this study, let us present the development of the arguments. It is designed more as a collection of essays exploring various aspects of the interlocking areas of social security and public choice rather than as an unitary analysis on one specific topic within this broad area. In principle, a conceptual distinction can be drawn between chapters 2 and 3, on one hand, and chapters 4 to 7, on the other hand.

Chapters 2 and 3 outline the main features of implicit debt, highlighting the analogies and the differences between implicit and explicit debt and defining the way in which unfunded obligations can be included in the existing public choice debate on funded debt.

The other chapters consider some allocational and distributional issues concerning unfunded obligations: the impact of demographic changes on their fulfilment (chapter 4); the features of the collective decision-making process using a median voter framework and the outcome of such a process (chapter 5); the role played by interest groups (chapter 6) and some empirical testing (chapter 7).

The results so far achieved allow for the drawing of tentative conclusions and provide interesting insights and fruitful lines of inquiry. A closer examination of the content of each chapter will provide a useful introductory framework.

1.2 Chapter 2 is concerned with the inclusion of pension obligations in a broad definition of public debt. Implicit debt, i.e. unfunded pension obligations, and explicit debt, i.e. funded interest bearing debt, are contrasted to outline the differences and the analogies which characterise these concepts. A wide concept of debt is not adopted simply for definitional purposes: indeed, the aim is to analyse unfunded pension obligations within the same theoretical framework used in the public choice literature to investigate the funded debt issue. Moreover, stressing the existence of an obligation, albeit implicit, does provide a conceptual framework for an investigation of individuals' perception of their pension entitlements and, as a consequence, their choices in the collective decision-making process.

Following closely upon these conclusions, chapter 3 describes the factors which affect individuals' perception of debt liability. Again, explicit and implicit debt are contrasted. The main argument is that ignorance, uncertainty, expectations, self-interest might lead, in both cases, to a systematic misperception of debt liability. The differences existing between these two forms of debt do affect their perception, too. For the unfunded case, the concept of "net social security liability" is introduced. The earmarked nature of social security contributions implies that the present value of the contributions paid will be compared with the present value of the benefits and that it is such a comparison which is the object of the individual perception, though no actuarial equivalence is guaranteed by the system. A systematic misperception, related to the individuals' ages, is likely to arise.

1.3 On the basis of the general arguments developed in chapters 2 and 3, more specific issues are dealt with in the other chapters.

More precisely, chapter 4 examines the impact of population changes on the fulfilment of social security obligations, using a theoretical model based on the premises of Baumol's Law. Basically, the idea is that, given a certain redistribution of income between retirees and workers, if the growth of population is such that the ratio between these two sectors of population is "unbalanced" (for instance, the former increases with respect to the latter) then, other things being equal, in order to fulfil the obligation, more resources have to be transferred from one sector to the other. This being the case, if individuals are allowed to choose their preferred contribution rate, assuming utility functions of conventional form, pension obligations are likely not to be fulfilled voluntarily. Different systems of fulfilment have different implications: if a system based on the fair sharing of "demographic risk" is chosen, population changes are likely to have less severe implications for the fulfilment of the obligation, when unfavourable demographic conditions do occur.

In chapter 5 the main features of a median voter-oriented collective decision-making process are exposed and a formalized model describing the median voter choice is presented. Having identified the median voter as the median aged individual, the specific application of such a model to an inter-generational redistributive problem, such as the pension issue, is discussed. The likelihood of the occurrence of a median voter outcome is explored and the constraints imposed on the median voter choice are made explicit. The main idea is that the level of pension fulfilment is determined by the median aged individual, taking into account the likely disincentive effects of an inflated level of fulfilment. Tentative suggestions toward this direction are derived from the model: the older the median voter (because of the occurrence of a decreasing population growth rate) the greater the utility deriving from an increasing contribution rate. Such a conclusion, however, does not necessarily hold when the likely disincentive effects exerted on the working population by an inflated contribution rate are introduced into the analysis.

Chapter 6 enlarges the analysis to take into account the role played by interest groups in the political process with respect to the pension case. This chapter is not meant to contrast rival theories but only to provide a picture as complete as possible of the features of the political process. And, indeed, it seems that the applicability of the median voter approach is not to be rejected when the existence of pressure groups is allowed for; only some notes of caution have to be introduced in predicting the political outcome. Basically, age would still remain the major factor influencing voters' demand for pension. However, the existence of many potentially different interests, the extent of which depends on the institutional features of the pension system, implies that different median voter demands might exist. Other things being equal (i.e. the population age structure) the interest group theory would imply higher demand for pension provisions. In other words, depending on the features of the real pension systems, if the interest groups play a relevant role, not only age but also intra-generational redistribution is likely to be a major determinant of the demand for pensions.

Finally, in chapter 7, an attempt at empirical investigation is carried out to test for the determinants of the demand for pension. It is not only the median voter and the interest group hypotheses which are examined; tests are also carried out for other hypotheses, such as the fiscal illusion and the voluntary redistribution hypotheses, both compatible with the demand-oriented approach developed in this study. Cross-section data, based on an OECD sample, as well as time-series data for Italy (1960–1984) are used. Regression results do not allow for drawing clear-cut conclusions; nevertheless, some arguments can be put forward. The median voter hypothesis receives support in both cases, while available data do not allow for accepting or rejecting the other hypotheses. The same equations perform better using time-series rather than cross-section data, probably because the latter are affected by the different socio-economic and political features characterising each country. Therefore, it is difficult to ascertain to what extent the differences in the demand for pension can be accounted for by the explanatory variables rather than by each country's socio-economic and political features. These considerations seem to provide support for the decision to deal with the pension issue also using a public choice approach, which seems suitable for grasping the complexity of the evolution of pension systems.

2. Notes on a definition of the concept of public debt

2.1 INTRODUCTION

2.1.1 The main purpose of this chapter is to provide a wide definition of the concept of public debt, including not only issued debt but also unfunded obligations, such as those deriving from a PAY AS YOU GO (PAYG) social security system.

The adoption of a wide definition of the concept of debt can be justified on analytical grounds and because of its economic implications. Both issues will be dealt with in the following pages. More precisely, in section 2 analogies and differences existing between funded and unfunded obligations will be examined in order to investigate the possibility that both obligations can be included in a theoretically correct concept of debt. The purpose is to explore the "contractual" aspects of the relationships underlying both obligations; therefore, government and individuals will be analysed, only in their roles of debtor and creditor, respectively. The "collective" dimension of such a relationship will not be taken into account. Once a wide definition of debt has been adequately established, section 3 will be devoted to an indication of the main economic implications deriving from such a definition, justifying the attention paid to this issue.

2.2 ANALOGIES BETWEEN BORROWING AND UNFUNDED OBLIGATIONS

2.2.1 As is well known, the terms "government debt" and "government borrowing" are often used interchangeably. According to this conventional view, public debt is generated only when the government issues bonds and withdraws saving from investors[1]. Basically, public debt is seen as relying upon the obligation government undertakes towards its creditors, i.e. the bondholders. Therefore, the concept of obligation is crucial for the definition of debt itself.

If we accept the existence of such a close conceptual link between debt and obligation and, indeed, it cannot be disputed there is no reason why the concept of debt should be restricted to borrowing alone; on the contrary, it might be extended in order to include other forms of obligation such as, for instance, those deriving from unfunded social insurance programmes[2]. In a PAYG system, the individual who pays his own contributions is entitled to receive the benefits, i.e. the pension,

5

only loosely related to the amount paid. Basically, as we shall establish later on, the entitlement to the pension derives from a peculiar obligation between the government and the worker, the former being responsible for the performance of the existing system. Therefore, both bonds and pensions are government debt, deriving from different types of obligation[3]. In the first case, government liability is represented by bonds and the debt is explicit; in the second case, being unfunded, it is implicit.

2.2.2 A relevant analogy does exist from the individual's point of view, too. For each individual, the acquisition of his "pension rights" through his contribution to a PAYG system can be equivalent to an act of saving[4], like the purchase of bonds, but compulsory and without any certain actuarial equivalence between benefits and contributions.

Moreover, another important analogy depends upon the fact that both have a relevant inter-generational as well as intra-generational redistributive impact. The ways in which such a redistribution takes place are complex and differ in the two cases, depending on the many specific features characterising these two forms of debt. These redistributive effects will be investigated in the following pages, where the differences existing between implicit and explicit debt will also be examined.

2.3 DIFFERENCES BETWEEN BORROWING AND UNFUNDED OBLIGATIONS

2.3.1 So far, the main analogies existing between funded and unfunded obligations have been sketched. However, before going on with an in-depth analysis it is useful to point out that a pure PAYG system is nothing but an extreme case which, eventually, is not always applied as a whole in reality. Indeed, many real social security systems, although based on PAYG principles, exhibit peculiar features somewhere between funded and unfunded schemes. Therefore, although PAYG is an interesting theoretical framework to which to refer, relevant policy insights can nevertheless be derived if a more realistic system (based on PAYG principles) is also taken into account.

Table 2.1 summarises the analogies and the differences which exist between funded and unfunded obligations: the first two columns draw such a comparison looking at the pure PAYG system whereas, in the other two columns, the U.K. pension scheme, taken as an example of a real social security system, is compared with borrowing. Moreover, the individual perspective is distinguished from the government perspective.

As we can see from the first and the third column, the same basic analogies hold in the two cases, although, as will be pointed out in the following pages, the extent of the redistributive effects in the U.K. system is likely to differ from that involved in a pure PAYG system.

Table 2.1. Unfunded government obligation compared with funded public debt.

| | PAYG System | | U.K. System | |
	Analogies	Differences	Analogies	Differences
Individual perspective (creditor)	form of "saving" yielding a return	1. compulsory saving 2. no counterpart in marketable assets 3. return on saving is not fixed	form of "saving" yielding a return	1. saving is compulsory but there exist alternative sources of supply 2. no counterpart in marketable assets 3. return on saving is not fixed
Government perspective (debtor)	redistributive effects future liability	4. existence of a plurality of interests among creditors, depending on specific personal conditions 5. the level of liability is not fixed	redistributive effects future liability	4. there exist a plurality of interests not only among creditors but also with regard to contracted out schemes 5. the level of liability is not fixed

2.3.2 Starting with the pure PAYG case, let us examine the differences between implicit and explicit debt. These differences are listed in column 2; they are far more than analogies. However, the existence of many differences does not alter the validity or the nature of the definition of debt outlined in this paper. In fact, once the main analogy, i.e. the existence of a future government liability, is accepted, the existence of many differences makes the inclusion of unfunded obligations within a wide definition of debt even more relevant. Actually, those differences imply equally disparate effects on contractors' behaviour and, as a consequence, relevant economic implications from the point of view of collective choice formation.

In table 2.1 differences are distinguished as follows: numbers 1, 2 and 4 hold only under the individual perspective, whereas numbers 3 and 5 represent two different aspects (from the point of view of the creditor and the debtor, respectively) of the same phenomenon[5]. Let us start with this last type of differences, given that it constitutes the general framework to which the others refer.

Differences 3 and 5 derive from the fact that the contractual relation underlying unfunded obligations is different from the one characterising government borrowing. Adopting the Williamson (1981) classification, the former seems to show some analogies with the complex category of *relational transactions* whereas the latter seems to fit into the category of *classical contracts*. The latter, as any usual market contract, is a discrete transaction[6] in which the nature and the features of the agreement are carefully delimited (amount borrowed, rate of return, maturity of assets, ...). Moreover, the identity of the parties may be considered irrelevant because it does not affect the performance of the contract. Therefore, although this type of transaction may differ slightly from market relationships because of the public nature of the borrower, the analogy still holds. Neither could it be otherwise; in fact, a government demanding funds is competing in the capital market[7] and it has to match the same structure which characterises market transactions.

On the other hand, unfunded obligations seem to be related to a different type of contract, resembling a "social contract". In fact, they come from a "social contract" existing between generations, which are linked because they belong to the same collectivity. According to this contractual relationship, which performs in a PAYG system, workers pay for financing retirees and, at the same time, accumulate credits toward future generations, benefits only loosely related to present tax payments[8].

Such a contract seems to be economically and politically profitable (at least, in theory): from the very beginning it provides the first generations of pensioners with benefits without imposing the burden on anybody else. In fact, the workers are requested to pay contributions which will generate future benefits. The same argument applies when, within the system, benefits and contributions are increased. Basically, through such a system, an income redistribution (between generations) takes place in each period; it is assumed to be "painless" for the contributing generation because it will be compensated by the redistribution that will take place in the next period. The only generation which is supposed to bear the cost of such a system is the last one because it would be requested to pay contributions without any repayment.

As Aaron (1966) pointed out, a PAYG system ensures a rate of return on the "invested" resources, and the financial independence of the system, as long as the real rate of interest is less than the sum of the growth rates of population and real wages[9]. In the opposite case, when demographic and economic trends do not allow for satisfying such a condition (see below, par. 2.3.4) the economic profitability of this form of investment is reduced and/or a financial crisis occurs in the system.

2.3.3 It is the "social" nature of unfunded obligations that gives rise to the differences indicated above.

Given their "social" nature, unfunded obligations do not arise from a discrete contract, with a fixed commencement, duration and termination, all these characteristics being present in the case of public borrowing. Any hypothesis of discreteness is fully displaced because the relationship refers to a society with a large array of norms, beyond those centered on the transaction and its immediate processes. Instead, it is an ongoing, long term relation which does not necessarily include any original formal agreement to which to refer, because it comes from a more general political agreement which anybody who is a member of a given society must accept.

Of course, there is a point at which the relationship comes into existence, but given its long duration and its complexity, the cost/benefit dimension of the formation stage does not seem to be of paramount importance. In fact, because of the existence of many specific interests, adjustment processes are likely to occur.

Then, the performance of the obligation will depend on the rules governing the relationship and determining the adjustments to the factors that will arise in the course of the relationship itself. Such rules are unlikely to be found in the legal system, the political market being the most suitable institutional structure to govern this relationship and its continuous adjustments[10].

Such adjustments do occur, either for strategic purposes or because of exogenous events (see below, par. 2.3.4); whatever the cause of adjustment, the effect is that uncertainty and flexibility are introduced in the performance of the obligation.

2.3.4 Let us consider more precisely how uncertainty and flexibility do occur. Generally speaking, uncertainty is an inherent feature of the contractual relationship, for there is always a lapse of time between the making of a contract and the promised performance. During that period a number of unforeseen contingencies may arise and may result in one party's failure to perform. Uncertainty is a critical dimension for a long-term and complex contractual relationship such as the one underlying unfunded social security obligations. Uncertainty mainly arises from factors depending on the debtor's behaviour (changes in legislation) as well as from exogenous factors (population and economic growth, changes in population age profile, ...). Both affect the return on saving for the creditor. On the other hand, the decision to retire is under the creditor's control[11] and ensures the flexibility of the return on saving (while it makes the amount of the obligation uncertain for the debtor). As a result, the amount of obligation (for the debtor) and the return on saving (for the creditor) cannot be rigidly determined when the contract is entered into.

The above considerations explain the origin of the differences listed under 3 and 5.

2.3.5 The only guarantee workers have for the fulfilment of the obligation rests on the government's power to tax the future working population to pay them social benefits. Given the social nature of this contract, social security being a means of socialising private obligations[12], the government serves as intermediary and political grantor for securing the performance of the obligation. It follows that although government is not formally primarily liable, it is, however, considered liable by the creditors given that the real debtor, i.e. the future generation, is hardly identifiable. Therefore, *de facto*, government is one of the two parties, the other being the collectivity of workers/taxpayers at any given time.

The identity of partners plays a more important role in this type of relationship than in the borrowing case; indeed, one of its most important characteristics is that it is embodied in the identity of contractors, without which it loses its specific meaning. In fact, although a social security system may not be the only method of ensuring an income stream to old people after retirement, the purpose to be served by the relationship, i.e. the socialisation of private obligations, seems to go beyond the actual object of the agreement. For this reason, once the original social scope is accepted[13], this kind of relationship has no adequate substitute: the creditor is locked into the transaction and the debtor is committed as well, because they cannot turn to alternative partners[14].

2.3.6 The identity of contractors is relevant because it helps to define the contractual relationship and the conditions of its fulfilment.

As far as creditors are concerned, it is interesting to point out that individuals are not parties to the contract on their own account but as members of a group (generation).

Since this group is very large, there exists within it a variety of narrow interests and, therefore, a great number of specific sub-groups which can try to gain benefits building up other specific contracts, on the basis of the original contract[15]. This mechanism is likely to give rise to the perverse effects which in the literature are referred to as the "isolation paradox" phenomenon: the uncertainty regarding other individuals' behaviour is an incentive for any individual to try to maximise his own specific interests without taking into account the costs of his action. The most important implication is that a systematic bias might be introduced in favour of the increase of benefits levels as well as of contribution rates[16]. Therefore, while in the case of borrowing, participation in the contract is on an individualistic basis, with the general purpose of getting a profitable rate of return on the invested capital[17], in the case of unfunded obligations, participation is also on a group basis and many specific interests are pursued.

This difference is useful for a definition of the way in which the intra-generational redistribution is realised in both cases. In the case of borrowing, the redistribution is in favour of bondholders and its burden is on taxpayers, i.e. it is well defined. To what extent this mechanism is regressive will depend on the characteristics of bondholders as well as on the kind of taxes used to finance the interest service.

On the other hand, the intra-generational redistribution realised through the PAYG system exhibits less precise characteristics. The pension is determined by the combination of many different elements and it makes it difficult to identify exactly the groups which are benefiting from such a redistributive process; therefore, it is not easy to determine if the system is progressive or regressive.

2.3.7 Looking at the identity of partners a problem arises, given that the state is a party to the contract, as well as the enforcer of the contract. Would people believe in its commitment? Would future legislatures be bound by the agreement, especially if the conditions of the obligation were dubious? The issue of fulfilment is made relevant by the fact that the timing of the streams of benefits and costs does not coincide and, therefore, the creditor's vulnerability is great because he incurs a cost before receiving a payment. Moreover, the external enforcement is imperfect because no legal remedies are provided if the government breaches the terms of the contract; the creditor can only rely on the other party's need for credibility[18].

In this specific case, the need for credibility is an important variable. In fact, political reputation is a necessary condition (although it is not sufficient) for any government to get consensus; indeed, it may be considered a link between different pieces of legislature ensuring continuity in the performance of the obligation. In other words, enforcement does not depend on economic transaction costs but on political transaction costs[19].

Generally, in *relational contracts,* the creditor is safeguarded only by the fact that the other contractor has to maintain his reputation and his credibility. In the unfunded obligation case, the need for reputation plays an important role, but its relevance differs from the private contracts context, where reputation is necessary for the survival of a firm in a competitive situation.

Some comments are in order. In the unfunded obligation case, competition does not exist because the State enjoys a monopoly position. The need for reputation can be justified only by recalling that politicians look for electoral success and, therefore, need to acquire voters' consensus. In this perspective, political reputation may be considered a link between different legislatures, ensuring continuity in the performance of the obligation. In other words, the fulfilment of the obligation does not depend on economic transaction costs but on political transaction costs. This situation differs from the one occurring in the case of public borrowing; in this latter case, in fact, a failure in government performance not only implies political costs but also bears economic consequences in terms of a weaker future position in the capital market.

The argument that the fulfilment of unfunded obligation is guaranteed by the need for political reputation may result in some criticism and needs to be further qualified.

First, a likely counter-argument is that voters are myopic[20] and, therefore, politicians do not need a long-term perspective like that required by the fulfilment of unfunded obligations. Following this line of reasoning, if we do not live in a world *à la Tiebout,* public choice theory would rule out the possibility that politicians would care about their long-term credibility. Therefore, if political decisions are for the short period only, the fulfilment of obligation is no longer guaranteed.

However, notwithstanding the possibility that politicians in taking their decisions do not try to ensure continuity with past political action, the fulfilment of the obligation is, at least partially, guaranteed by the need for political consensus, in the present. In other words, if unfunded obligations are not met in full, the consequences will be borne by creditors in the present and, therefore, the present political fortune of a government producing such damage is likely to be affected as well.

This argument does not completely guarantee the fulfilment: in fact, the final outcome cannot be defined *a priori* because it depends on the comparison between the political relevance of young generations (who are likely to refuse to honour burdensome unfunded obligations) and that of retirees (who will support the fulfilment). Therefore, even if, in principle, the argument based on the need for political reputation still holds in the short term, the fact that conflicting interests are involved makes any *a priori* forecasting difficult.

2.3.8 So far, the issue of uncertainty in the fulfilment of unfunded obligations has been dealt with and no attention has been paid to the welfare implications coming from such uncertainty. Some comments are in order on this last issue.

The fact that creditors are not fully guaranteed does not imply only negative evaluations; in fact, it can also be considered as a form of "protection" for future generations.

If the fulfilment were certain, this would imply that future generations would be compelled to pay for an obligation which was not undertaken by themselves and the fulfilment of which may become extremely expensive, because of the existence of demographic and economic factors and owing to the mechanism underlying collective decisions. Moreover, certainty would also prevent any search for a more efficient system to provide aged people with support. As Parsons and Munro (1977) point out, the question arises whether it is desirable to favour a system that provides considerable windfalls to one generation and considerable losses to another, subject purely to changes in the birth rate.

This issue has not only theoretical but also practical relevance. In fact, the current discussion on social security systems has been conducted in the context of rising concern over the soundness and fairness of the PAYG system, because of the existence of unfavourable economic and demographic trends, leading most social security systems into a state of financial crisis[21]. A strong political and theoretical debate rages on this issue: various objections have been raised to the PAYG system, calling for its reform[22].

A solution for restoring the stability and viability of the system can be found in an adequate reformulation of the underlying contract. According to Musgrave (1981) the problem is one of structuring the system so that the implicit contract can be adhered to by each generation: a viable system calls for an inter-generational contract that provides for a fair sharing of the risks caused by uncertain future changes in productivity and population growth. Currently, the burden is placed on the working generation, endangering the viability of the system over time. As a solution to this problem, Musgrave proposes that contributions and benefits be adjusted so as to maintain a constant ratio between per-capita earnings (net of contributions) of the working population and per-capita benefits of the retirees. Such a formula would result in a fair sharing of risks with regard to uncertain productivity and population changes[23].

In such a situation the fulfilment of the obligation mainly depends on the political evaluation of the competing interests and of their relative relevance. Therefore, the previous conclusion is confirmed, even if adequately qualified: unlike the case of public borrowing, the fulfilment of unfunded obligations depends only on the evaluation of political costs, as a result of offsetting contributors' interests against beneficiaries' interests.

2.3.9 Having defined the different nature of the contractual relationship underlying public borrowing and unfunded government obligations, let us consider how the other differences listed in table 2.1 fit this picture.

Because of the "social" nature of the contract, individuals are compelled to "save" in order to finance the system; this means that this form of saving is not necessarily profitable for them. It can become profitable only under specific circumstances either exogenously determined (the above mentioned economic and demographic factors) or created by the parties' behaviour, through a process of bargaining.

This situation differs from the one occurring in the borrowing case. In fact, as Buchanan (1958) argues "if an individual freely chooses to purchase a government bond, he is presumably moving to a preferred position"[24]. Therefore, in this latter case, the bargaining, if there is any, is only *ex ante* and not *ex post*.

The second difference related to this form of saving is that it is not represented by any marketable asset. This feature may have at least two very important consequences. Firstly, it affects individuals' economic behaviour, constraining, for instance, their chance of borrowing, and narrowing the range of economic choices they face in the present; however, although it has a relevant economic impact[25], it does not seem to affect the political process. Moreover, the absence of any visible asset may conceal the very existence of this kind of debt[26].

In summary, having described the main differences and analogies existing between borrowing and unfunded obligations, the initial hypothesis, i.e. the possibility of including both in a wider definition of debt, seems viable. In fact, both imply a future government liability and lead to present expenditure; the existing differences, basically related to the differing nature of the respective contractual relationships, do not alter this fundamental analogy.

2.4 THE U.K. PENSION SYSTEM CASE

2.4.1 With respect to the above analysis, some interesting differences emerge, when the U.K. system is taken into account. They are listed in column 4.

In the U.K. system it is possible to contract out of the earnings-related component of the state scheme[27], though membership of the basic component is compulsory. In the case of contracting out, both employer and employee pay reduced rates of national insurance contributions. In return, the private scheme

14

must provide a "Guaranteed Minimum Pension" (GMP)[28] which is to be subtracted from the employer's state pension entitlement.

At the same time, the 1986 Act allows guaranteed minimum contribution (GMC) or money purchase schemes, which make no commitments on final benefits, to receive the same rebate on National Insurance Contributions. Moreover, according to the 1986 Act individuals will be able to contract out of the state's or their company's earnings-related scheme and have a rebate on national insurance contributions paid directly into their own personal pension. Contracting out does not in itself modify a worker's pension entitlement; it only implies that part of such entitlement will be met by a private scheme. Looking at the table 2.1 (columns 3 and 4), let us briefly sketch how the above analysis can be related to this system.

2.4.2 Uncertainty (i.e. differences under 3 and 5) does exist, but in a different perspective.

From the government point of view, liability is still uncertain. The effects of contracting out on long-term costs depend on whether, in a steady state, the loss for contribution rebates is more or less than the annual savings from the occupational scheme. The effect of contracting out also depends on the magnitude of this phenomenon. As Dilnot and Webb (1988) point out, the impact of the changes introduced in 1986 is very difficult to assess. This impact will unfold over a period of many years and until the new system has been in operation for some time it will not be possible to know how many individuals will switch out of the state scheme[29].

In summary, if the above considerations hold, with respect to the pure PAYG case, no major changes are introduced in terms of the uncertainty of government liability. Indeed, uncertainty still holds and, to a certain extent, it might be enhanced by the fact that the contracted out schemes are offered the option of ceasing to contract out and giving their obligations back to the state (according to specific provisions).

From the creditor's point of view, no relevant differences are introduced by the option of contracting out given that, as has been pointed out, workers' entitlements are not modified. Therefore, the uncertainty regarding the return on saving seems to hold in the same terms as in the pure PAYG case.

2.4.3 With respect to the other differences listed in table 2.1 a few comments are in order. Social security obligations still represent a form of compulsory saving which, however, can take different forms. The existence of alternative "sources of supply" is likely to enhance individuals' incentives to obtain information about the pension issue: if this is the case, an unsatisfactory state performance in the fulfilment of social security obligations is likely to bear more relevant political costs. For this reason, the "need for reputation" may play a more important role (although not at the same level as in the *relational contracts*) than in the "pure monopoly case".

At the same time, the scope of political bargaining is enlarged in the sense that other groups, representing the vested interests of various occupational and private schemes, enter the bargaining process. Given that occupational schemes are *regulated* (i.e. some schemes must provide a minimum guaranteed pension; the rebate on contributions is defined and so on) the details of this regulatory activity are also a matter of bargaining. Therefore, the difference n.4 not only holds but is even more relevant than in the pure PAYG case, because, when contracting out (and for that matter ceasing to contract out) is allowed, other actors enter the scene and new specific interests are likely to be pursued.

2.4.4 Moreover redistributive effects might derive from the above mentioned features of the U.K. system, among the other things depending on the impact of contracting out on the contribution rate of non-contracted out employees. The direction and the extent of these effects depend on the scope of contracting out as well as on its qualitative features, i.e. on the "identity" of contracted out workers.

In summary, the proposed wide definition of debt seems to fit also into a more realistic PAYG system, such as the U.K. system. The analysis needs to be better qualified: the intra-generational as well as the inter-generational redistributive issue should be explored adequately and alternative institutional solutions for funded schemes might be investigated and compared. However, such a development is outside the scope of this work, whose purpose is only to stress that the proposed wide definition of debt fits into real pension systems, the U.K system representing an example. Therefore, pensions represent an implicit government debt, the amount of which is uncertain, which is likely to enhance the political bargaining among specific competing interests and imply a significant intra-generational redistributive impact.

Leaving aside the further investigation of these complex issues, let us consider which policy implications are likely to stem from the proposed wide definition of public debt.

2.5 ECONOMIC AND POLICY IMPLICATIONS

2.5.1 A first relevant implication of the wide definition of public debt proposed above is cognitive. In fact, considering both implicit and explicit debt allows for defining a measure of government size in the present and in the future, which is as realistic as possible. The wide-ranging discussions existing in many countries on the size of the public debt, its growth and its control would stress the relevance of a better knowledge of the economic aggregates under consideration[30]. Relying on a wide concept of debt is a way of knowing what amount of resources the govern-

16

ment has to repay and, further, its likely size in the future. However, to stress the relevance of this "knowledge" should not lead to an underestimation of the difficulties underlying the measurement, or rather the forecasting of unfunded obligations[31]. In fact, the quantitative dimension of this kind of debt seems to be more difficult to assess than that related to the interest bearing debt. Any estimate is highly conjectural, because of the above mentioned degree of uncertainty characterising this form of obligation, future liability depending on future legislation as well as on demographic and economic changes. However, far from giving a precise measurement of government liability, a wide definition of debt is likely to offer useful insights in this direction.

2.5.2 Moreover, a wide definition of debt is also interesting under a public choice perspective. More precisely, the joint analysis of both implicit and explicit debt may offer a better understanding of the bargaining process characterising the political market and of the role played by public debt in this context.

Following this approach, the range of items, dealt with by the bargaining underlying the political-economic equilibrium, is enlarged: not only present expenditure but also future expenditure and, therefore, not only a tax/debt mix but also a more complex mix composed by taxes, present obligations for future expenditure and present obligations for present expenditure. This means that more degrees of freedom are faced by the actors in the political market and that the outcome of the bargaining becomes more uncertain, depending on the differential impact of each item on the individual's behaviour. The uncertainty is also enhanced by the various dimensions of unfunded obligations mentioned above as well as by the existence of many specific interests which leave room for bargaining on the performance of the obligation itself. Indeed, the existence of such sectorial interests, coupled with uncertainty, is likely to give rise to a strong "isolation paradox" problem, affecting the individual's perception of public activity costs and expectations on the bargaining outcome.

Indeed, a wide concept of debt is likely to be helpful in an analysis of the individual behaviour within the fiscal illusion theory. The argument that borrowing may be used to affect the perception of voters and taxpayers and, therefore, to influence the outcome of the political process[32] has to be recalled and widened: in this case, not only debt *per se* but also its complexity are to be considered strategic means. Basically, considering unfunded obligations as public debt might serve to extend the argument that politicians tend to reduce the "visible" size of debt, making its structure as complex as possible[33]. In the light of these considerations it seems reasonable to conclude that a wide definition of debt is helpful for an understanding of the complexity of the political decision-making process underlying fiscal decisions.

NOTES

1. The various theoretical aspects involved in the public debt issue have been examined, among the others, by Cavaco Silva (1977) and by Buchanan, Rowley and Tollison (1987). Since the fifties (and in line with the XVIII century debate) there has been a great deal of discussion about the so-called problem of "equivalence" between debt effects and tax effects. On this wide issue, see chapter 3.

2. Pensions, which are the main object of this study, constitute only one of the social security programmes. In fact, as is well known, social security can be defined as a set of different programmes providing for cash payments or curative services when deficiency in earnings or physical disability arises: programmes for a) old age, invalidity and survivors; b) sickness and maternity; c) work injury; d) unemployment benefits and e) family allowances.

3. The theoretical analogy between unfunded obligations and borrowing has not received much attention in the literature except for Peacock (1986), Castellino (1985), Rizzo (1985) and, only vaguely, Buchanan (1983) and Browning (1973). Some authors (Boskin, 1982; Hills, 1984) recognising such an analogy, draw attention to the methodological problems related to the measurement of the wide concept of debt deriving from this analogy (on this issue, see, below, par. 2.3.1). From the accounting point of view, there is no unique definition of unfunded debt: Castellino (1985) and (1987a) suggests making it equal to the present value of future benefits contractually implied by the PAYG obligation. Such a definition, however, would imply that unfunded debt does arise even if the PAYG system is balanced. Alternatively, allowing for such a problem, the debt deriving from unfunded obligations should be considered equal to the present value of future benefits minus the present value of contributions.

4. The question whether "social security saving" can be considered a perfect substitute for funded private saving has not been answered unambiguously in the literature; indeed, the answer is crucial in assessing the impact of social security on individual propensity to save. In fact, social security would be expected to decrease saving to the extent that workers consider social security benefits a substitute for funded personal saving; on the other hand, it would not have any effect to the extent that social security benefits are considered a substitute for other forms of public sector or intra-family transfers to the aged. In this latter case, older generations would react by increasing bequests to the younger generations. Feldstein (1974) and (1976a) estimated the effects of social security on saving to be negative and substantial. Stronger depressive effects have been recently identified by Bernheim (1987). Moreover, the extent of social security impact on saving is likely to be reduced if the "retirement effect", implying that social security as a whole diminishes the labour supply of the elderly (see, below, note 11), is taken into account. Surveying the literature, Aaron (1982) contends that there is no consensus about the effects of social security on saving and that the empirical work to date has largely served to produce "a series of studies that can be selectively cited by the true believers of conflicting hunches." (p.51). It is interesting to note that the debate on social security effects shows strong analogies, *mutatis mutandis,* with the discussion about the public debt effect. Such analogies have been stressed by Feldstein (1976b) and Barro (1974).

5. Any rigid classification is arbitrary and over-simplified; however, once one is aware of its limits, it can be useful to analyse the various dimensions of a concept, especially when these dimensions are closely related, as in the case under consideration. Within this context, to say that a difference holds from the creditor's or the debtor's point of view means only to stress that its consequences affect *mainly* and *directly* either individual or government behaviour, without denying that the other party will be affected too. In fact, these political actors interact and, therefore, indirect effects are likely to occur.

6. Discreteness holds in the contractual relation with any single bondholder (interest

bearing debt is usually refunded) whereas it is less sharply defined in the borrowing activity considered as a whole. However, the existence of discreteness in each single contract allows for a precise definition of the amount of the obligation.

7. Government can reduce such competition through fiscal devices (for instance, tax exemptions for returns on public bonds) which make public bonds more attractive to investors. Moreover, the "publicness" of the borrower may introduce another interesting difference in this kind of contract. In fact, apart from the polar and unrealistic case of not repaying its debt, government can implicitly reduce the real value of such debt, without violating any contractual rule, by creating inflationary pressure.

8. This is the case when pensions are related to earnings (variously calculated). The actuarial equivalence is ensured in a system where benefit levels depend on the amount of contributions paid during working life.

9. Aaron uses the significative expression "social security paradox" to describe the functioning of this system. When these conditions hold, the PAYG system is more attractive than a reserve system. The comparison between these systems is a major controversial issue and its analysis is outside the scope of this study; for a discussion, see Thompson (1983).

10. The political market is defined as the arena where competing political parties attempt to achieve power, trading policies with votes (see, Peacock,1979).

11. In the literature, it is debated whether social security affects retirement decisions in the sense that it stimulates early retirement. Boskin (1977a) and (1986), and Munnel (1974) argue that the level of social security benefits offer incentives to retire; Burtless and Moffitt (1984) place less emphasis on this effect. Indeed, no clear cut conclusions are reached on the size of this effect but it is widely recognised that some features of the pension systems, such as, for instance, the "earnings test", can enhance it.

12. The idea that social security socialises private obligations relies upon the concept of a family including two or three generations and providing mutual insurance and self-protecting functions, the essence of the family being the sharing of resources and systematic inter-generational transfers. Social security, merely socialises transfers from workers to their parents and transfers are channelled to the elderly in this way, rather than through an extended family. Recently, Becker and Murphy (1988) have explored such an issue, getting the conclusion that government intervention in family decisions (subsidies to education, social security and old age support) contribute to the efficiency of family arrangements.

13. This scope of social security is not commonly agreed; for a discussion of this wide issue, see Boskin (1977b).

14. This effect derives from the specificity of the asset; the object of the transaction, in fact, is not saving itself but saving as a tool to express inter-generational solidarity. In a wider context, Williamson (1979) stresses the importance of asset specificity which limits the ease with which one or both parties can terminate the relationship and seek a substitute performance.

15. Age of retirement, family situation, indexation methods, ceilings on contributions and benefits are some of the parameters that specific interest groups can use as objects of bargaining with government. Such bargaining activity enhances the extent of intra-generational redistribution involved by social security. On this issue, see chapter 6.

16. This systematic bias is stressed by Browning (1975). However, a different conclusion can be reached if the disincentive effects of high contribution rates are taken into account in the political decision-making process. Such an issue is addressed in chapter 5.

17. Individuals' aptitude should be analysed in a more complex framework where not only the "contractualistic" dimension of borrowing is considered but also its role as a means of financing public spending. This public choice dimension of borrowing has been explored by Buchanan (1964b) and, more recently, by Carter (1982) and Ganderberger (1986). Indeed, it is with respect to this public choice dimension that a wide concept of debt might provide the most interesting insights (see, below, par. 2.5.2).

18. As Goldberg (1980) points out, generally speaking, the non-coincidence of the streams of costs and benefits is immaterial only when the weak party either has cheap effective legal remedies available or can rely on another party's need to maintain his reputation.
19. Enforceable promises require that some transaction costs be positive, otherwise contracting parties would breach the contract too easily, because doing so would be costless (see Goldberg, 1980).
20. For a broad perspective on this issue see Frey (1978).
21. One of the most easily identifiable trends in Western Europe as well as in the United States is the increase in the age component of the population coupled with declining fertility rates. According to some estimates (see, for instance, Rix and Fisher, 1982), in the future, fertility rates are likely to increase only slightly whereas age trends are not supposed to change. The consequence of such a demographic scenario is the growth of transfer payments to an increasing number of retired workers. Such demographic impact on pensions has been estimated by Byatt (1986) for the U.K., by Lynn (1983) for the United States and by Ministero del Tesoro (1986) and INPS (1987) for Italy. Comparative estimates are provided by Tamburi (1983) and, more recently, by CER (1987) and by Halter and Hemming (1987).
22. On such a debate, with specific reference to the United States, see Boskin (1986), Kotlikoff (1987) and Weaver (1982). On the debate on the Italian pension system, see the contributions by Artoni, Castellino and Morcaldo, published in Politica economica, 1987, n.1.
23. This issue is further developed in chapter 4.
24. This issue is further developed in chapter 3.
25. The impact may be relevant to the propensity to save (on this issue, see above, note 4).
26. To make this debt explicit, Buchanan (1968) suggested the issue of non-transferable social insurance bonds, these bonds being the identifiable claim on the government of entitlement to retirement income support.
27. The current arrangements of the state retirement pensions are defined by the Social Security Act 1986. The Act introduced major changes to the system of earnings-related benefits (aimed at reducing its generosity) as well as to the structure and level of both state and private pension provisions. Most changes do not affect those retiring in the state scheme until the next century. A detailed description of such a reform is outside the scope of this work (see Dilnot and Webb, 1988; and Creedy and Disney, 1988) only some major features, relevant for our analysis, will be pointed out here. More precisely, according to current legislation, the pension is earnings-related and consists of two components: the *basic component* (which is flat-rate) and the *additional component* (which is earnings-related). The former is equal to the lower earnings limit; the latter is a percentage of average lifetime earnings.
28. The GMP is roughly equal to the additional state pension; it is based on average lifetime earnings and is inflation-adjusted up to 3 per cent per year, with any excess inflation adjustment financed by Government.
29. With respect to the system existing before 1986 Hemming and Kay (1982) calculate a small reduction of state's liability.
30. On this issue, see Boskin (1982) and (1987), Byatt (1986) and Hills (1984).
31. These difficulties are stressed by Eisner (1984), Eisner and Pieper (1984) and Castellino (1985)..
32. Such an argument is supported by Buchanan and Wagner (1977).
33. This issue is extensively explored in chapter 3.

3. The public debt perception issue

3.1 INTRODUCTION

3.1.1 In the previous analysis the theoretical reasons underlying a wide definition of public debt were investigated and the analogy existing between bonds and unfunded obligations was stressed: in both cases the government borrows in the present with the promise of giving back the money plus the interest in the future. Thus, the role of both obligations as a means of financing government activities was not adequately explored. The following analysis is aimed at investigating this issue from the specific point of view of the individual's perception of fiscal burden. More precisely, the purpose of this chapter is to include unfunded obligations in the framework of public choice analysis.

Unfunded obligations considered as a means of financing public expenditure show some peculiarities that may justify the attention paid to them. Assuming the existence of an ideal spectrum of fiscal devices ranging from taxation to borrowing, they can be assumed to fall somewhere in the middle: they imply a present tax liability (as taxation does) in an inter-temporal context (like borrowing). Moreover, while in the debate on borrowing, attention is usually focused solely upon future tax liability, in the case of unfunded obligations future benefits also become relevant. In this case the taxpayer's time horizon refers not only to the tax liability but also to the benefit side, owing to the specific features of these obligations. These characteristics of unfunded obligations are likely to influence individuals' perception of government fiscal activity. Considering these obligations as a fiscal device might introduce interesting qualifications with respect to the public choice debate on fiscal illusion and, more generally, with reference to the political market outcome.

In the following sections some of the several questions raised above will be examined and a few tentative conclusions will be offered. More precisely, in section 2 a brief survey of the current debate on debt illusion will be presented; in section 3 the fiscal perception issue will be investigated with respect to the funded debt and in section 4 it will be extended to include unfunded obligations and the differences existing between these two cases will be outlined. The likely policy implications stemming from the individual perception of unfunded debt will be pointed out in section 5 and dealt with in the next chapters.

3.2 PUBLIC DEBT ILLUSION: A BRIEF OVERVIEW

3.2.1 Broadly speaking, within the public choice context it is commonly accepted that the voters' demand for public expenditure is strongly affected by the means of financing such expenditure because of the occurrence of fiscal illusion. The central theme of this literature is that the institutional manner in which citizens are required to pay for government is likely to affect the taxpayers' perception of the price of government activities; more precisely, some government financing tools are costly to be perceived and, therefore, using these methods will, *ceteris paribus,* decrease the perceived price of collective activities[1] and modify voters' preferred levels of outlay. In a median voter model of collective choice the effect is assumed to be an undue expansion of the public sector[2].

The fiscal illusion idea, although stated in a different context, goes back to Puviani (1903) who argues that ruling authorities attempt to create optimistic illusion by making citizens feel they are taxed less and receive more than is actually the case. This theme has been extended to modern democratic settings by Buchanan (1964a) who stresses that elected governments find it advantageous to design tax structures that make voters think that they pay less onerous taxes than is actually the case.

3.2.2 Deficit financing is considered an important source of fiscal illusion. Again, Puviani suggests that public debt is a means of making the cost of government appears to be less than it is. According to him, taxpayers are assumed not to perceive the tax liability involved in the debt issue. Moreover, he suggests that government tends to reduce the "visible" amount of outstanding debt, making its structure as complex as possible, giving rise to a proliferation of securities with different maturities and interest rates.

Analogously, according to Buchanan and Wagner (1977), the replacement of current tax financing by government borrowing has the effect of reducing the perceived price of governmental goods and services, what they call the "relative price" change. This does not necessarily imply that citizen/taxpayers do not anticipate the future tax liability related to government borrowing but only that they do not value it at the extreme limit. As Buchanan and Wagner point out, "to the extent that the costs of governmental goods and services are perceived to be lowered by any degree through the substitution of debt for tax finance, the relative price change will be present". This relative price change embodies an income as well as a substitution effect. Buchanan and Wagner emphasise the latter; according to them, debt financing reduces the perceived price of public expenditure and, in response to this effect, citizens/taxpayers increase their demand for these goods and services.

3.2.3 In general, the fiscal illusion hypothesis has been widely questioned even among those who accept the public choice theoretical postulates on the grounds that while misperception must be permanent in order to have any significant effect on the level of spending, there is no reason to believe that voters will permanently misperceive their tax burden (Gandenberger, 1986) because this would postulate a succession of short misperceptions and, therefore, imply absence of learning.

Moreover, as Carter (1982) has pointed out, even if individuals are likely to underestimate their objective tax burden because of the costs involved by the perception of tax institutions, it does not necessarily follow that their "subjective" image of that burden is also altered. Assumptions have to be made about the individual transformation of objective information of costs into subjective estimates of such costs.

Furthermore, a distinction has been drawn between misperceptions of the total and of the marginal burden. It is claimed that even if the total burden is underestimated (because it is permanent) the same argument cannot be used to justify the underestimation of the marginal cost. In fact, the habituation effect does not apply to marginal costs. However, it has been recognised (Carter, 1982) that some financing methods, such as public debt, can generate misperception of both total and marginal tax costs.

3.2.4 Indeed, the issue of debt illusion is relevant not only *per se* but also because it can be considered the core of the endless controversy on the "debt neutrality" thesis[3]. The issue of debt neutrality has been dealt with from two different points of view; either looking at the debt finance effects on the level of aggregate demand or at its effects on the level of public expenditure, within a public choice framework. Although these effects refer to quite distinct economic problems, their common root lies in the individual perception of public debt. As Niskanen (1978, p.592) points out,"federal deficits either reduce the perceived tax price of federal services *and* they stimulate aggregate demand or they have no effect on either federal spending or aggregate demand". In this paper, attention will be paid to the public choice aspect.

3.2.5 If the "neutrality" thesis is accepted, i.e. if debt is recognised as having identical effects to taxation, then the argument of debt illusion in itself loses any significance. No clear-cut conclusion can be reached on strictly theoretical grounds; in fact, this is more than a theoretical issue, it is an empirical one. The existing evidence is far from conclusive; however, the empirical findings provided with respect to the effects of debt on the aggregate demand cast some doubts upon the "neutrality" hypothesis[4];on the other hand the empirical evidence on the public choice aspect, i.e. the effects of debt financing on the level of public output, is highly controversial and needs further investigation[5]. This chapter is not aimed at resolving this debate; its purpose is only to try to explore the issue further, trying to answer some objections raised against the fiscal illusion argument, as far as funded and unfunded public debt are concerned.

3.3 FUNDED DEBT PERCEPTION

3.3.1 As is highlighted by a consideration of the above issues, in public choice literature criticism of the concept of fiscal illusion, its behavioural assumptions and its theoretical implications has often led to a denial or at least to a criticism of the hypothesis that citizens are likely permanently to misperceive certain features of government activity. Sometimes, such a criticism seems to stem from the fact that an implicit, though not justified, parallel is established between the concept of illusion and the idea of irrational behaviour. The fact that many economists are unhappy with any deviation from the perfect rationality hypothesis, traditionally underlying economic theory, has led to a rejection or to an underestimation of the relevance of the fiscal misperception issue.

The question is not without importance. To the extent that misperception, whatever its causes, affects individuals' behaviour considered as actors in the economic and political markets the revenue and expenditure decisions of democratic government as well as the nature and the level of economic activity will be influenced. Therefore, the concept of fiscal perception should be considered crucial in any analysis of the individual as well as of the collective decision-making process.

On the basis of these considerations, and before examining the specific issue of funded debt perception, it seems interesting to explore the concept of illusion in more general terms, especially as far as its analytical relationship with the concept of rationality is concerned.

3.3.2 The existence of fiscal illusion implies a distortion in the taxpayer's choices. Because of the occurrence of such a distortion, he will undertake actions that he would not have undertaken if he was aware of the fallacies altering his representation of existing alternatives. Therefore, in the presence of illusion, the alternative ordering is not incoherent *per se* but only if it is compared with a situation where the above mentioned distortions had not taken place. It follows that if the mechanisms generating illusion are known, it is possible to arrive at a systematic analysis of illusion itself. Once the individual's aims are known, as well as the nature of his illusion, his decisions can be anticipated and studied systematically[6]. It is in this respect that illusion differs from irrationality.

This issue recalls a central tenet of the methodological dispute in economics based on Simon's theory of *bounded rationality*. Simon (1955), (1959), (1972), (1976) supports the hypothesis that *procedural rationality* is relevant in economics in contrast with the more traditional *substantive rationality* approach. The former approach is concerned with *how* decisions are made rather than, as in traditional economics, with *what* decisions are made. In other words, Simon stresses the fact that individuals do face limits in putting into practice their objectives. These limits depend upon their ability to evaluate, their organizational capability and are, in general, psychological as well as social limits. Therefore, the normal condition can be assumed to be the imperfect knowledge of available alternatives and their outcomes. Because of the above mentioned individual limits and because of the uncertainty of outcomes, anybody who wants to behave rationally is bound to build up a simplified and manageable model of the real situation. It is with respect to this model that the individual behaves rationally, though such behaviour is not optimal with respect to the real world. The individual's behaviour, therefore, is likely to follow an alternative ordering which is different from the one which would be adopted if he had a perfect knowledge of reality, i.e. in the absence of the above mentioned limits. As Giardina (1965) points out, the analogies between fiscal illusion and *bounded rationality* are relevant: in both cases there are choices which are optimal in terms of perfect rationality and choices which are optimal only with respect to the individual representation of reality. In order to study the latter type of individual choices, it is necessary to study how the factors limiting individual rationality actually operate and how the individual builds up his simplified model of reality.

The following analysis is not aimed at pursuing such an ambitious aim but only at providing some insights leading to an identification of the factors affecting the perception of debt future tax liability and to asses whether there are systematic sources of misperception[7] in this specific field.

3.3.3 Debt illusion arises as a consequence of errors in individual understanding and evaluation of taxes implied by debt. As Cavaco Silva (1977, p.37), suggests, "public debt illusion, related to future taxes that an issue of debt represents, should be defined in terms of the degree to which individuals do not perceive accurately the total of future taxes that a public borrowing contractually implies and which will have to be paid by members of the present community or by their heirs". Therefore, according to this definition, debt illusion is an illusion in the sense that is usually given to this term: a phenomenon that appears to be what it is not.

To explore the debt illusion issue it seems useful to focus attention upon two different elements. On the one hand, there are some features of funded public debt – its complexity, the vagueness of the taxes to service it, its quantitative dimension and its diffusion among the savers which may affect the taxpayer's perception of debt tax liability. On the other hand individuals' perception of the stream of future taxes involved in the issuance of debt[8] is affected by many factors, existing separately and interacting together. Uncertainty, ignorance, rational self-interest and expectations[9] seem to be the most relevant, at least given the features of funded debt. The combined effects of these different elements on debt future tax liability perception are summarised in table 3.1.

Table 3.1. Public debt future tax liability perception.

Debt features	Sources of perception			
	Ignorance	Uncertainty	Expectations	Rational self-interest
Complexity of the debt structure and of the discounting procedure.	The existence and the issuance of many forms of securities with different maturities and interest rates makes it difficult to acquire perfect information of total and marginal debt and of aggregate tax liability.			
Unlegislated debt service taxes.		Individuals, ignoring which tax will service the debt, are not able to define their personal future tax liability.		
Size of outstanding debt and present tax liability to service it.		The magnitude of outstanding debt and the present tax liability to service it can be used as indicators of permanent tax increases, unless a debt self-reproduction mechanism occurs.		
"Democratisation" process (i.e. eventual coincidence between boldholder/taxpayer roles).				The profitability of debt might induce individuals to take into account the debt "net tax liability".

3.3.4 Ignorance is likely to be caused by the high costs of acquiring information. These costs, in turn, are likely to be a function of the complexity of the debt structure (many forms of securities, different maturities). In the presence of a high degree of complexity it may even be inconvenient for individuals to become informed.

Indeed, the debt case is just one of the several economic situations characterised by imperfect information and no attempt is made here to explore such a controversial issue. Just to sketch the nature of the problem it is important to stress that in these situations it is not easy for the individual to identify the optimal level of information[10]. Such a calculation should be based on the crucial assumption that it is feasible to know exactly what kind of information will be obtained by a specific information-gathering act. This is not a realistic assumption. Information, is a sought-after commodity; one presupposes that the value of information is unknown because if the content of a piece of information was known, it would not have been demanded. In cases such as these, economic theory fails to come up with an analysis of what might be considered optimal consumer behaviour. Following Atkinson and Stiglitz (1980, p. 299) it might be argued that imperfect information leads "into areas that are far from fully treated in the case of private economy. We cannot, therefore, appeal to a widely accepted body of theory and much of the discussion is qualitative in nature".

Going back to the specific case under study, let us undertake a closer examination of public debt and imperfect information. Imperfect information is likely to refer to outstanding debt as well as marginal borrowing, in the sense that an individual might not even be aware of the exact amount of outstanding debt and/or of the issuance of "new" debt. Indeed, unlike the tax case, there is no *a priori* reason to believe that the marginal tax liability involved in the issuance of a new debt will be better perceived than the total outstanding debt tax liability, given that, by definition, it is not realised in the present.

Moreover, even if he is aware of these events, the individual might not necessarily be able correctly to measure his own debt future tax liability : the imperfect information about the actuarial equivalence concepts, as well as the difficulties of applying them (what interest rate has to be chosen?) might induce him to make a wrong evaluation of future tax liability. Ignorance about the debt issuance , may give rise to debt illusion[11]: if individuals are not aware that the debt has been issued, they will not be able to anticipate any tax share.

3.3.5 Furthermore, even if individuals know that the debt has been issued and that it will involve a stream of future taxes, it still does not follow that they will be aware of their own future tax shares and be able to measure them correctly. The neutrality hypothesis rests on the idea that debt is serviced by a lump-sum tax; relaxing such an unrealistic condition, certainty about individual future tax liability does not hold any more. Indeed, when debt service taxes are not legislated in advance, it is hard to identify the future individual tax liability.

The fact that, in practice, it is impossible to know which taxes are going to be levied to service the debt does not necessarily imply the existence of illusion with respect to the aggregate debt future tax liability. In fact, even if the specific taxes used to service the debt are not known in advance, the individual can still be aware of the total amount of tax required.

3.3.6 Moreover, the perception of debt future tax liability is affected by individuals' expectations: the magnitude of borrowing, its rate of change and especially the tax liability incurred in the present to service the existing debt can be taken as indicators of future deficits and borrowing and, therefore, of permanent future increases in tax liability.

Individuals' projections of future benefits and taxes are likely to be erroneous. Such errors are consistent with rationality. In fact, each individual utilises and processes all the available information; as we said before, such information is not always accurate. The important question is whether these errors will be systematic, leading to over or underestimations of future tax liability. No clear-cut conclusion can be reached on this specific issue. In the extreme case of a debt self-reproduction mechanism (new debt is created to service the existing one) the learning process would be delayed through time and individuals, not being asked to pay taxes to service the debt, would not be able to form expectations about debt future tax liability. Therefore, this phenomenon, would allow for the existence of a permanent delay of the tax liability perception deriving from the fact that, instead of levying taxes, new bonds are issued to service the existing debt. In other words, the individual on the grounds of available information might *correctly* be induced to believe that no tax liability is involved in government debt[12].

3.3.7 Lastly, it seems important to stress the fact that in the presence of debt, individuals might potentially be both creditors (lenders) and debtors (taxpayers) simultaneously. This phenomenon is likely to influence their perception of the tax liability deriving from deficit financing as compared with tax financing.

Indeed, the coincidence of savers' and investors' roles seems to occur in most industrialised countries, where the phenomenon of "democratisation" of debt has taken place[13]. Such a phenomenon can be explained by saying that citizens are encouraged to buy government bonds by the greater convenience which is usually ensured by such a form of financial investment (either because real rates are higher than for analogous alternative private forms of investment or because of the existence of fiscal privileges on bonds' return). Following the same line of reasoning, it might be argued that if government securities were not convenient,the "democratisation" process would not have taken place[14], the argument recalling Buchanan's proposition (1958) that an individual purchases a government bond because he expects to be better off by doing so. The behavioural impact exerted by this "two-fold" identity[15] on individual attitudes toward government spending cannot be defined with certainty. Nevertheless, some insights may be derived from the above mentioned "democratisation" process itself, as far as individual preferences for different means of government financing are concerned.

As a consequence of such a process, when comparing debt financing and tax financing, rational self-interested individuals (taxpayers and savers/lenders at the same time) would look not only at their debt future tax liability but at their debt future "net tax liability" (NTL)[16]; i.e. the present value of future tax liability is likely to be evaluated net of the greater convenience derived in the present from financial investment in bonds compared with other forms of financial investment.

3.3.8 The concept of NTL deserves some comments and may be questioned from different points of view. That *at the margin* government bonds are perceived as more convenient than private securities is proved by the fact that savers voluntarily choose to buy them. It follows that savers can be considered to be better off when government bonds are issued than when they do not exist. Therefore, they are likely to consider debt financing more convenient than tax financing since the former offers opportunities for investing their saving which would not exist if the latter system of financing was used.

It might be argued, however, that in this comparison loans to the private sector are to be taken into account as an alternative to public loans. As already pointed out, a central tenet of the "equivalence" hypothesis is that the effect of the government's replacing the tax with the public loan is nothing more than the replacement of a whole set of private loans with a single public loan. Now, for the private lender, provided that the interest rate of public debt is higher than the interest rate of private debt, the economic convenience of tax financing and debt financing will differ[17].

Indeed, there is no *a priori* reason to believe that public debt is necessarily more convenient than private debt; lenders, in fact, do not face both simultaneously and, therefore, the argument that they prefer public debt cannot be assessed on an *a priori* basis. From this point of view, the concept of NTL might seem to lose relevance: lenders might consider both means of financing as equivalent. On the other hand, however, it cannot be disregarded that the extent of such an argument is likely to be limited by the increasing utilisation of public debt as a means of ordinary finance. Borrowing, in fact, should be compared with ordinary taxes rather than with some once-and-for-all tax and in this case the analogy between private loans and public loans might not necessarily hold. Therefore, bearing in mind this framework, the concept of NTL would still seem worth considering. Furthermore, another question might be raised. It might be objected that the voluntary purchase of government securities does not necessarily demonstrate that individuals do benefit as a consequence of the debt issuance. According to a rational expectations argument, recently recalled by Shaw (1987, p. 194) "within the context of a multi-holding setting, any household not purchasing debt in period 1 will be involved in a distributional transfer in favour of bond-holding households in period 2, when the debt is redeemed, since the revised tax burden does not discriminate between the bond and non bond-holding private sector. Each household will possess an equal incentive to acquire debt".

The argument, however, while suggestive, requires further qualification. First, doubts may be cast upon the hypothesis that debt future tax liability can be fully capitalised. This general argument, however, refers to the assumptions rather than to the content of the objection itself. Looking at this latter issue, it should be pointed out that it does not explicitly take into account the financial opportunities which are an alternative to public debt. Even if the costs and benefits related to the purchase of government securities are in balance for the "ultra-rational" private sector, the individuals' perception of such a balance may be affected when bonds are considered as an alternative to other securities. Unless we assume that a unique interest rate does exist – and this is not necessarily the case, as the empirical evidence shows – individuals are likely to compare the opportunities offered by the capital market. In this respect, the argument that they buy bonds because they are aware of the future redistributive process initiated by the bond issuance does not seem persuasive. It appears to be unlikely that they will disregard eventual more convenient alternatives[18]. Therefore, government securities have to be, at least as convenient as the other securities offered in the market.

Some other questions arise. Firstly, it is not clear why the government should issue bonds if individuals are indifferent between different sources of revenue[19]. Furthermore, if no explicit convenience is introduced with respect to other securities, no guarantee exists that the required revenue can actually be raised by issuing bonds unless the "ultrarational" household behaviour described above is considered realistic by government. Indeed, such a scenario does not seem to fit with reality. The overall question of "equivalence", far from being clearly defined, requires further explanation.

The rationale of the NTL argument is that it does not matter whether individuals fully discount their tax liability. In the event, because of ignorance and uncertainty with respect to future taxes levied to service the debt, a correct evaluation is unlikely to occur. Moreover, when a debt self-reproduction mechanism occurs, any evaluation based on the information available in the present would lead to an underestimation of debt future tax liability. However, even if the unrealistic assumptions of certainty and full information are considered to hold and permanent tax increases are correctly foreseen, still, *ceteris paribus,* deficit financing and tax financing are likely to make a difference: in the former case, the NTL is likely to be taken into account.

The more pronounced is the "democratisation" process, originating in the relative convenience of state securities with respect to other forms of financial investment, the more mixed are the taxpayers'/bondholders' roles and the more likely it is that individuals, even perfectly discounting their own future tax liability, will look at their NTL.

3.3.9 Further support for this argument can be derived by recalling the argument recently stressed by Friedman (1985) that, under conventional circumstances, increasing the market supply of an asset is likely to raise that asset's market-clearing expected return. Transferring this argument to the public debt case, the strength of the hypothesis based on future NTL appears to be greater, the more accurate is the individual's information about debt issuance.

If an individual is fully aware of the amount of debt issued, his expected return on bonds will increase, in absolute as well as in relative terms, and, as a consequence, his perceived NTL will be lower. The extent of this effect, as far as the relative expected return is concerned, depends on the degree of substitutability between bonds and other assets[20] and is a matter for empirical investigation, depending on the characteristics of financial markets. What is important is to stress the fact that full information and awareness of debt issuance might work against equivalence, in contrast with the conclusions reached in the literature, once the NTL concept is taken into account.

In other words, one might argue that there exists a demand for bonds, depending on the rate of return and on the individual forecasts about the future tax liability they involve. As a consequence of the above mentioned factors, it is likely that the debt tax liability will be underperceived when compared with tax financing liability (the size of this misperception being related to the size of the democratisation process). This phenomenon does not necessarily imply any irrational behaviour or any misperception of the stream of future taxes deriving from servicing the issued debt.

3.3.10 The argument just outlined, the extent of which depends on the size of the democratisation process, has implications for the outcome of the collective decision-making process, when the level of government has to be chosen. If the idea is accepted that debt financing is not regarded by taxpayers solely as a cost, being at the same time a profitable form of investment, it follows that voters' reactions against debt and tax financing implying equal "gross tax liabilities" will differ. The former is likely to be weaker than the latter, at least as long as public debt ensures a higher rate of return than other forms of financial investment. Therefore, the price of debt-financed expenditure will be perceived as lower than the price of tax-financed expenditure.

Any citizen, as an investor, is likely to support the debt creation because, in this case, he benefits from a specific transfer programme, the cost of which will be borne by the collectivity of taxpayers. However, the fact that individuals, as bondholders, support government activity by providing financial resources voluntarily does not necessarily mean that they agree on the level of deficit-financed expenditure and, more in general, on the growth of government.

At least two hypotheses can be formulated: either they agree with the size and the growth of government spending, underperceiving its cost (given that NTL is discounted) or they choose to subscribe to the debt as a convenient form of financial investment, without agreeing with the size of government.

The former hypothesis recalls conventional debt illusion theory, although differently motivated. The latter deserves some comments. It can be explained by recalling the "isolation paradox". A majority of taxpayers might prefer a reduction of public debt (and, therefore, of public activity) but they might be uncertain whether expressing their preference in this sense (i.e.not buying bonds) would result in a corresponding reduction of government activity or, instead, in an increase of taxation. In other words, any utility maximising individual will try to exploit a convenient form of investment, the cost of which is borne by all members of the community.

On the other hand, it is likely that the government will stress the profitability of its debt: using debt finance, the government jointly supplies public expenditure, whatever it is, and a specific transfer programme, i.e. debt interests, to a large share of the population, whose size increases as long as the "democratisation" of debt develops.

To sum up, the arguments briefly outlined above would suggest that the misperception hypothesis seems to gain support as far as the funded debt is concerned. Let us consider how the above considerations on debt perception can be extended to the unfunded obligation case.

3.4 UNFUNDED DEBT PERCEPTION

3.4.1 In a consideration of the unfunded obligations perception issue, the first point to be made is that the object of perception itself ought to be better specified, in line with the arguments just developed for the funded case. The idea of taking into account a "net liability" deserves some attention also for the unfunded debt, though it cannot be extended without adjustments to this case. Let us define such a concept more carefully; the comparison with NTL will throw some light on this issue.

The essence of the "net liability" argument lies in the fact that individuals are assumed to evaluate their tax liability (in this case, their social security contributions liability) not in isolation but in relation to the future benefits they receive from contributions. In fact, although in a PAYG system no actuarial equivalence is assumed to exist between contributions and benefits, entitlements nevertheless arise, and are seen to arise, as a consequence of the pension obligation itself.

Strictly speaking, in a PAYG system, from a budgetary point of view, social security contributions are paid to finance present pensions; however, from the taxpayer's point of view, these contributions are paid to finance his own pension, i.e. future expenditure. This latter perspective is crucial for the essence of the contractual relationship underlying unfunded obligations. Because social security contributions are earmarked taxes, it is likely that not only present tax liability but also the present value of future social security benefits will be taken into account. For this reason, from the individual's perspective, the link between social security taxes (paid in the present) and retirement benefits (to be received in the future) is likely to be strongly perceived, given that today taxpayers are also creditors for future benefits tomorrow. This is the first difference arising between the funded and the unfunded case. In the funded debt case, in fact, the benefits of the bond-financed expenditure were not taken into account; since it was non-earmarked borrowing, such a link was not easily identifiable. Moreover, even if this were the case, taxpayers and beneficiaries would not necessarily have been one and the same. In fact, borrowing could be used to finance very specific spending programmes, the benefits of which accrue only to narrow categories of taxpayers.

On the other hand, just because of the earmarked nature of social security contributions, the link between the present tax liability and the present value of future pension benefits is likely to play a relevant role in determining the individual's perception. As a consequence, the individual's behaviour in the collective decision-making process, for instance, the demand for pension, will also be affected. Therefore we might say that the object of the individual's perception is the "net social security liability" (NSSL). From such an individual perspective[21] NSSL can be said to arise only when the estimated present value of future benefits is lower than the present value of the contributions paid or, in other words, when the actuarial equivalence does not hold.

3.4.2 Having identified in very broad terms the likely object of individual perception in the unfunded debt case, let us explore such a concept in more depth. It might be argued that the above definition is somehow reductive. It assumes that the individual does not look for alternative ways of investing his "social security saving" and, therefore, implies a "passive adjuster role" on the part of individuals. If this is the case, the intellectual problem might arise of why an individual, locked into the social security contract, should care about evaluating the NSSL. The cost related to such an action would probably exceed the benefits[22]; the larger the group deciding for social security, the lower the individual's incentive to get involved in the pension issue.

Following this line of argument one might conclude that when an alternative does exist, or is perceived to exist, the comparison between two different ways of investing the "social security saving" would encourage the individual to seek to understand the system and to require a level of pension provision at least as convenient as that ensured by private funded pension plans. Indeed, the alternative might be hypothetical rather than actual: the comparison would be drawn between the rate of return ensured (or forecasted) by the PAYG system and the financial investment opportunities offered by the capital market.

In such a situation the concept of "net liability" would refer to the opportunity cost of joining a public pension scheme compared with the rate of return otherwise obtainable by private pension schemes or in the capital market, if the individual were allowed to contract out or to reject the obligation[23]. In other words, NSSL could be defined as the rate of return ensured by the PAYG system (as determined by assessing the present values of contributions and benefits) net of the higher (or lower) return obtainable by alternative financial investment[24]. Such a wider definition of NSSL recalls the reasoning underlying the concept of NTL: again, a comparison between the funded and the unfunded cases may be helpful.

A crucial consideration in the definition of NTL was that the taxpayer/saver was able to *choose* whether to buy bonds or, more generally, government securities instead of other assets because of their convenience. The situation is different when pensions obligations are taken into account. In fact, given that they are compulsory, they are undertaken regardless of their convenience. Therefore, in the unfunded debt case, it is questionable whether the perception of NSSL might be seen as depending on the comparison between the rate of return obtainable within the PAYG system and that provided by alternative private systems. In other words, such a wider perspective, though interesting, might seem highly abstract. It assumes that individuals are willing to bear the costs of getting informed about alternative pension provisions even if they are not allowed to choose any alternative. On the other hand, it provides useful insights for an exploration of individual behaviour when facing decisions about the level of social security contribution rates (and, therefore, of pension provision) or about the existence of the system itself (and, therefore, the fulfilment of existing obligations)[25].

The above considerations would suggest that neither of the two definitions just described is to be preferred on *a priori* grounds. Nor are they mutually exclusive, the latter being just a development of the former. The former is more reductive but more realistic, especially when no alternative private pension schemes exist. The latter is more suggestive, though more unrealistic, unless real possibilities of choice exist for taxpayers.

Actually, the adoption of either of these two concepts is not crucial for the following analysis: having established that the link between social security contributions and benefits is the basis of NSSL, awareness of the fact that individuals might be concerned with the *relative* convenience of the system simply adds a further qualification to the analysis, without questioning the relevance of the link between social security contributions and benefits. The institutional features of different systems strongly affect the relevance of the two concepts just put forward.

Table 3.2. Perception of "Net social security liability".

Unfunded debt features	Source of perception			
	Ignorance	Uncertainty	Expectations	Rational self-interest
Complexity of benefits structure.	The fact that benefits are computed on a personal basis makes it difficult to acquire information about their aggregate amount but not with respect to the indiviual amount.			
Characteristics of contributions structure and collection.	The splitting and the witholdings of contributions makes it difficult and costly to assess their amount with respect to the aggregate as well as to the individual amount.			
Complexity of the discounting procedure.	The lack of the understanding of the concept of discounting and the difficulties of applying it makes it difficult to evaluate the present value of taxes and benefits.			
The features of the unfunded obligation fulfilment are indeterminate.		Individuals will not know the lenght of their life. The return on contributions is uncertain and crucially depends on government behaviour in the future.		
Level of social security in the present.			High degree of fulfilment in the present would suggest high future contribution (to be paid by future generations) and high future benefits.	
Full coincidence between lenders and taxpayers through time but not at any given point in time.				An asymmetry in perception arises in relation to the age: only part of voters, the lenders (i.e. the workers) perceive the NSSL; as a consequence, their economic behaviour is adjusted. NSSL perception is likely to vary with workers' age.
Contracting out options.				The return obtainable from the PAYG system is compared with alternative private systems.

3.4.3 No matter which definition of NSSL we adopt, some differences between NSSL and NTL deserve to be stressed.

From a merely taxonomic point of view it should be pointed out that while the NTL refers to future tax liability and present benefits, the NSSL implies future benefits and present tax liability. This issue might deserve attention only if relevant differences are assumed to exist in the discounting process, as far as its application to taxes and benefits is concerned.

More interesting differences arise when the extent of such a concept is taken into account. In the funded case the relevance of NTL depends on contingencies such as the size of the "democratisation" process; in the latter, since all the population is covered by the PAYG system, the evaluation of the link between social security contributions and benefits as well as of the PAYG system cost opportunity refers to the overall population. Nevertheless, differences arise across the population depending on age. More precisely, only one generation, i.e. the working generation is the subject actually perceiving NSSL each time; retirees, having already paid taxes in the past, can be assumed to play a "passive" role in each period as far as the perception of NSSL and the related collective decision-making are concerned[26].

3.4.4 In analogy with the analysis developed in section 3, let us consider what the main unfunded obligation features which affect the perception of NSSL are (they are summarised in table 3.2).

In order to avoid misunderstanding, it is better to point out that tables 3.1 and 3.2, although apparently similar are not comparable. The reason lies in the fact that NSSL and NTL have different extent, the former referring to the overall population. Both concepts refer to debt creditors: however, in the former case such a group is defined by law, given that joining the PAYG system is compulsory, while in the latter purchasing government debt securities is voluntary and, therefore, potential and actual bondholders are not one and the same. It is true that such a difference would be minimised if contracting out was feasible in the pension case. However, the element of compulsion is not likely to be eliminated, at least for the minimum pension level. Because of such a difference, which is inherent in the nature of these two forms of debt, the extent of NTL and NSSL varies as well.

Thus, NSSL can be considered the object of fiscal perception for the total working population and, therefore, the combined effects of uncertainty, ignorance, etc. and the debt features are taken into account with respect to such a concept. In fact, the title of table 3.2 is "Perception of net social security liability". On the contrary, NTL refers only to a segment of the population and, at present, occurs because of the specific features of funded debt, namely the "democratisation" process. Therefore, table 3.1 does not refer to the perception of NTL, and in fact its title is "Perception of funded debt future tax liability". Bearing this difference in mind, let us look at table 3.2 more closely.

3.4.5 As well as in the funded debt case, the complexity of the social security system makes it difficult to acquire perfect information. In this case, however, ignorance may refer also to the individual liability, given that it depends on decisions which are taken in the present. Legislation being unchanged, individuals are potentially able to determine their NSSL. What is uncertain is whether such a value will be maintained through time (see following section).

Lack of information is not likely to occur with respect to personal benefits. Since this is a very specific issue, individuals will probably be well informed either personally or because of the existence of "organised information" (in connection with pressure groups, unions,...).

On the contribution side, the fact that contributions are split into employer and employee portions may probably affect the perception of individual tax liability; indeed, in the literature it has been claimed that individuals are not aware either of the employer portion or of the fact that it constitutes a burden for them. Moreover, even the portion paid by the employee is not likely to be easily perceived, being withheld at source. Therefore, one might argue that NSSL misperception is likely to arise more on the cost side than on the benefit side.

On the other hand, in an aggregate perspective, the misperception deriving from the lack of information will refer to contributions as well as to benefits. The main reason is that information is costly. In fact, benefits are calculated on the basis of a wide range of specific and highly personal parameters (age, pre-retirement income, family status...) as well as on the basis of complicated legislation designed to meet specific groups' interests. Therefore, the aggregate amount of future benefits is not likely to be correctly perceived. On the contributions side, the same arguments outlined above hold, and probably with more force.

3.4.6 In the case of unfunded obligations, uncertainty refers to government behaviour and to personal variables as well. Uncertainty regarding the length of life as well as future health conditions will make uncertain the present value of future benefits (i.e. the return of the obligation) which strongly depends on age and on the length of retirement. At the same time, given that no legally enforceable contract underlies the obligation, its fulfilment is uncertain (is government likely to force future generations to fulfil the obligation even in presence of unfavourable demographic and economic conditions?) This uncertainty depends on the fact that government may change its identity and nature.

NSSL perception is affected by expectations, too. The size of the existing system will be taken as an indication of the future size of the system. In this case, expectations mainly concern benefits, given that social security contributions are paid in the present[27]. It should be noted that in this case expectations do not necessarily play a pessimistic role; a high degree of fulfilment in the present, i.e. high pensions, might suggest that the system will ensure a satisfactory "return" in the future, too.

3.4.7 Finally, it is interesting to note that the necessary coincidence through time of the roles of taxpayer and creditor also implies that perception (or misperception) is likely not to be equally distributed among the individuals. The crucial determinant of such a distribution would seem to be age.

In the case of general taxation, fiscal perception depends upon personal variables (for instance, education, income, etc...). Some differences do arise in the case of PAYG unfunded obligations. Social security contributions are earmarked taxes levied on workers and yielding benefits only to aged people; in this case, then, at any given point in time, part of the population, i.e. the retirees, will not perceive any cost because they are not requested to face it[28]. Given the definition of NSSL (regardless of the existence of private alternatives) such a concept refers only to the working generation, i.e. to the overall group of creditors. However, even the part of the population which pays, i.e. the workers, the unfunded debt creditors, is likely to perceive NSSL differently according to age. The youngsters will probably concentrate more on the contribution side whereas middle-aged people will have more incentive to seek information about the benefit side. Therefore, even within the working generation some will be more interested in perceiving the contributions while others, being near to retirement, will be more interested in perceiving the benefits. The same asymmetry, depending on age, holds if the hypothesis of contracting out is taken into account. However, in such a case as was pointed out, the object of creditors' perception would be NSSL in the wider sense described before[29], i.e. as the difference between the net return deriving from the PAYG and the return obtainable from other private financial alternatives.

3.4.8 On the grounds of the above considerations, an asymmetry in perception is likely to arise with respect to both the contributors and the beneficiaries. This being the case, NSSL is likely to be misperceived and the degree of such misperception will probably depend on the age of the population.

Leaving aside the NSSL perception and looking at an aggregate perspective, a difference with respect to the funded debt case ought to be stressed: at any given point in time, in the unfunded case, only part of the population plays the lender role and faces a tax liability while in the funded debt case a part of the population lends but the whole collectivity faces a future tax liability. This means that, in terms of collective perception, the asymmetry is likely to be more pronounced in the unfunded case, for the funded debt depending on the relative weight of bondholders with respect to the overall population, i.e. on the extent of the debt "democratisation" process. It is an asymmetry, however, which rests on the coincidence of different roles, implying different rational interests, within the voting population. The argument needs, of course, further investigation, given that the extent of this source of misperception is an empirical matter. The implications stemming from the above considerations will be dealt with in the next chapters.

3.5 CONCLUDING REMARKS

3.5.1 In this chapter, different possible sources of fiscal perception were taken into account. The main conclusion stemming from the analysis is that misperception is likely to occur in both funded and unfunded cases. Relevant differences do arise between these two cases highlighting the fact that, although both types of debt imply the existence of an obligation, their implications to the political economy differ.

The first difference pertains to the object of perception. In the funded debt case taxpayers will evaluate not only the debt future tax liability but also its rate of return: the higher the latter, when compared with the rate of return ensured by the market, the more favourable will be the taxpayer's attitude toward public debt. As a result, adopting a strictly individual perspective this would lead to an extensive coincidence of the roles of bondholders and taxpayers. The underestimation of debt tax liability is likely to occur, the object of perception being NTL.

In the unfunded debt case predictions are less straightforward. Two main features characterising this form of debt ought to be stressed: the earmarked nature of social security contributions and the full coincidence between lenders' and taxpayers' roles through time. It follows that the link between contributions and benefits holds for all the working generation (i.e. the creditor) and it is the difference between the two, i.e. the NSSL, which is the object of perception. Age plays a relevant role in affecting such a perception, in the sense that middle-aged workers will be more interested in information and more aware of benefits rather than costs. A systematic underestimation of NSSL might result from the ageing of the population. Nor should it be overlooked that the contributor is more likely to be badly informed than the beneficiary; this also leads towards the underestimation of NSSL.

At the same time, also within an aggregate perspective, the perception of the pension burden is likely to depend on the age of the population, an ageing population being more inclined to its underperception. The above conclusions are only tentative and require further investigation: however, they would suggest that there is room for exploring the political economy implications of age as far as unfunded obligations demand and fulfilment are concerned.

NOTES

1. The costs of obtaining information on the individual fiscal burden are assumed to vary according with the different kinds of public revenue items and the institutional structure of the revenue system (modes of tax assessment; elasticity of the tax structure, Craig and Heins, 1980; complexity of the revenue system, Pommerehne and Schneider, 1978).
2. This traditional public choice argument holds on the assumption that expenditure

benefits are correctly perceived. If this is not the case, voters might be subjected to mutually exclusive misperceptions with no effect on public spending demand.

3. As is well known, the tax/debt controversy centres around the question of whether taxation and debt are similar in their real effects. The argument underlying the "debt neutrality" hypothesis is that when a government uses debt finance instead of tax finance, expectations of additional future taxes of equal present value offset the current tax reduction, so that the timing of tax liabilities does not matter (Barro, 1974). On the other hand, others argue that the two methods differ mainly because of the occurrence of fiscal illusion, and that, as a consequence, the issuance of debt instead of taxation causes potential saving to fall. The "debt burden" is then shifted to the future in the form of a lower capital stock. For a survey of different positions, see Ferguson (1964), Buiter and Tobin (1979) and Holcombe, Jackson and Zardkoohi (1981).

4. This conclusion has been reached with respect to the United States (Feldstein, 1982 and Boskin and Kotlikoff 1985), Italy (Modigliani, Jappelli and Pagano, 1985 and Modigliani and Jappelli, 1987) and using international samples (Koskela and Viren, 1983 and Kessler, Perelman and Pestieau, 1986). For different results, see Kormendi (1983) and Barro (1989).

5. Few studies attempt to test for the debt illusion hypothesis (see Niskanen, 1978; Shibata and Kimura, 1986); the difficulties related to this kind of analysis are stressed by Peacock and Rizzo (1987).

6. Therefore, the traditional distinction between rational behaviour and illusion loses significance given that both can be studied in a systematic way.

7. The words misperception and illusion will be used interchangeably.

8. Debt can be issued either to finance an increase of expenditure, taxation being unchanged, or to counterbalance a tax cut, expenditure being unchanged. The latter is the conventional hypothesis underlying the debt equivalence debate (see Buchanan, 1976). In terms of individuals' perception, within the specific perspective of this section, concerned with funded debt, it does not seem to make any difference which one of the two hypotheses occurs. Only if debt was issued to finance a specific expenditure, would individuals' perception be affected, debt perception being joined to the evaluation of the benefits deriving from expenditure (see section 3.4). In all the other cases, when debt is issued to finance general government activity, individual perception of debt future liability is likely not to differ from that arising when debt is a substitute for a tax cut.

9. These factors are not homogeneous: uncertainty derives from the characteristics of reality and is somehow out of the individual's control; ignorance, rational self-interest and expectations pertain to individuals' behaviour and to their interaction with a given reality.

10. Following the usual optimal consumer behaviour principle, information should be accumulated as long as the cost of an additional effort to collect information falls short of the maximum willingness to pay for the additional information.

11. The idea of considering ignorance as a source of debt illusion is not unanimously agreed in the literature. Cavaco Silva (1977) argues that public debt illusion applies only to those who are not ignorant of the debt issuance which contractually implies taxes, otherwise the expression seems to him misused. Indeed, this argument deserves some attention. Strictly speaking, the necessary condition for a misperception is that the issue to be perceived is known. However, unless we assume the occurrence of complete ignorance about the debt phenomenon, considering imperfect information as a source of misperception can be, at least in principle, justified. In fact, if the taxpayer knows something about the existence of funded public debt, the decision of not acquiring further information, i.e. if it increases or decreases, implicitly contains an evaluation of the different aspects of the problem and, therefore, implies a process of subjective understanding which may in turn be in error. On this ground, and because of the difficulty of drawing clear-cut distinctions in such difficult area, it seems better to consider ignorance a source of illusion. Such a simplification does not have any effect

upon the analysis itself.

12. Within the framework of a rational expectations approach such behaviour might be questioned because it assumes that agents ignore future events. However, it might be argued that agents are not actually in ignorance of and do not understate future events but only provide an interpretation of the consequences deriving from these events, this interpretation being formed in the light of their past experience. On the other hand, as Spaventa (1988) points out, a debt self-reproduction mechanism, might lower the credibility of State's solvency and, therefore, savers' demand for bonds.

13. De Viti De Marco (1939) used this expression to denote the case where households invest their saving to buy government securities. This phenomenon is quite widespread in most western countries. For instance, in Italy, the share of state debt held by households has increased through time during the last decade: the Treasury, supplying debt instruments with high real yields and liquidity shifted the bulk of the debt ownership from banks to the non-banking public. Spaventa (1984) points out that in contrast to Barro's hypothesis no systematic changes in the saving ratio occurred, despite the mounting stock of debt. The growth of state debt appears to have affected the composition rather than the size of assets held by the public. As Bollino and Rossi (1988) show, in the period (1960–1986) the composition of households' net wealth appears to have changed, a substantial shift having taken place from currency, bank and postal deposits to government securities. Onofri (1988) points out that the size of the fiscal illusion phenomenon tends to decrease as long as the amount of public debt increases.

14. The argument that government debt is profitable refers to a limited time horizon and is based on the idea that the government correctly services its debt. This assumption might not necessarily hold in a very long-term perspective and/or under specific circumstances, such as war debts. This point was stressed by Pareto (1917, p.135), although in a different context. According to him, the equivalence issue "assumes that governments will service their debts. This can be considered true for a not too long period of time. It is not true when centuries are involved ... Debts are a means of exploiting those who have the illusion of being repaid".

15. This coincidence of roles seems to be more evident when short-term bonds are issued. However, if we allow for the interdependence of utility functions between generations the debt maturity loses any relevance from this specific point of view.

16. The concept of NTL has been explored by Rizzo (1988). The macroeconomic implications of public debt and its eventual displacement effects are assumed not to be taken into account by individuals in the evaluation of their own NTL. Indeed, such effects are highly controversial and no clear cut conclusions have been reached in the literature as far as the debt effects on economic growth and national income are concerned; therefore, no systematic individual bias can be anticipated in either direction. A comparison between debt financing and tax financing "burdens" has been drawn by Feldstein (1985).

17. In the literature (De Viti De Marco,1939) the opposite phenomenon has been examined, i.e. that government is able to borrow at an interest rate lower than the capital market rate because of its solvency. Such a situation would lead to "non-equivalence" too, though from a different perspective, the debtor's perspective. In fact, taxpayers would prefer to pay the taxes for servicing public debt rather than to borrow money (at a higher rate) to pay the extraordinary tax. Also in this perspective, "non-equivalence" holds not for the population overall but only for those (employees, autonomous workers) who, because of lack of liquidity, have to borrow money to pay the once-and-for-all tax. A similar argument, though in a more modern setting, has been put forward by Barro (1974). Whether the creditor's or the debtor's perspective prevails is a matter of empirical investigation.

18. Nor should it be overlooked that while the individual future tax liability is uncertain, given that the debt is not serviced by lump-sum taxes, any difference in the financial convenience ensured by different securities is not affected by the same uncertainty and

is more clearly perceived.

19. A similar argument has been put forward in Peacock and Rizzo (1987).

20. The expected return on assets that investors regard as close substitutes, for example, government debt and high grade corporate debt of comparable maturity, presumably move closely together. On the other hand, if investors do not regard two assets as close substitutes, an increase in the market supply of one can lower the expected return on the other. Empirical studies carried on in the USA by Friedman (1985) show that government financing raised expected debt returns relative to expected equity returns, regardless of the maturity of government's financing.

21. This argument holds only for the individual liability perception and not for the aggregate liability perception, (i.e for the aggregate social security burden). Indeed, the individual might be interested in evaluating the amount of unfunded debt to be repaid in the future but, in this case, he is likely to look at the entitlements acquired in the present for obtaining the pension in the future. On this basis, legislation being unchanged, he can estimate the amount of resources which in the future are to be transferred to pensioners. In other words, the perception of the aggregate social security debt liability is not affected by the concept of NSSL. This does not mean that the aggregate liability is not relevant for the individual. Indeed, its relative magnitude affects the possibility of future fulfilment and, therefore, the willingness to pay in the present. This issue will be explored in chapter 4.

22. The benefits consist of the gain eventually deriving from the political participation activities undertaken to demand individual as well as collective improvements in the level of pension benefits. Such a gain is likely to be greater the larger the number of specific pension schemes (this issue is examined in chapter 6).

23. The hypothesis of the rejection of the obligation is explored in chapter 4.

24. Once such a definition of NSSL is accepted, the use of the word "liability" itself can be questioned. In fact, NSSL is expected to exhibit a positive value when PAYG is more convenient than alternative systems and, as a consequence, negative when such a convenience does not hold. In other words, the sign of NSSL is counter-intuitive. However, notwithstanding such inconvenience, for the sake of terminological continuity, it seems preferable to use the expression NSSL to label the object of individual perception in the pension case.

25. The issue is explored in chapter 4.

26. This does not imply that retirees do not perceive any NSSL: indeed, they will compare the present value of contributions paid in the past with the value of benefits accruing in the present. The fact is that they cannot do anything but partecipate in politics to defend their entitlements and/or to achieve new privileges (see chapters 5 and 6). Saying that only the working generation is the relevant segment of the population as far as NSSL perception is concerned simply means that, at any given point in time, the liability determined by a PAYG system is borne by working generations and, therefore, it is how they perceive such a liability that matters when decisions about unfunded obligation fulfilment are to be taken. Only workers, being the productive sector of the population, can alter the value of NSSL (for instance, by reducing their work effort).

27. This argument holds in a strictly individual perspective. As has been pointed out in note (21), in an aggregate perspective a high degree of present fulfilment combined with unfavourable economic and demographic projections, might lead individuals to form pessimistic evaluations of the future possibilities of fulfilment. The implications stemming from this issue are examined in chapters 4 and 5.

28. In other words, given the amount of contributions paid in the past, retirees look only at the benefit side.

29. See paragraph 3.4.2.

4. The fulfilment of unfunded obligations and the problem of population growth: An application of Baumol's Law

4.1 INTRODUCTION

4.1.1 In chapter 2 it has been pointed out that implicit and explicit debt, although they have in common the fact that they are based on an obligation, differ quite substantially in the way in which such an obligation is defined. Government unfunded liability is uncertain because it depends on factors which are exogenous (economic growth, population growth, age profile) as well as endogenous to the contractual relationship (decisions about retirement, changes in social security legislation); therefore, no precise definition of such a liability can be included in the contract.

In this chapter attention will be paid to the impact of demographic changes on the fulfilment of social security unfunded obligations. Baumol's Law throws new light on such an issue. Basically, the idea is that given a certain distribution of income between retirees and workers, if the growth of the population is such that the ratio between these two sectors of population is "unbalanced" for instance, the former increases with respect to the latter then, other things being equal, in order to fulfil the obligation more resources have to be transferred from one sector to the other. The extent of such a transfer is likely to vary according with the method of fulfilment. The different effects exerted by alternative systems of fulfilment will be explored and the policy implications stemming from them will be outlined.

A simple model will be set up to illustrate the application of Baumol's Law to the social security issue. Moreover, the way in which different systems of fulfilment generate different problems will be outlined.

4.2 THE MODEL

4.2.1 This section will be devoted to build up a simple model to explore the impact of ageing on the fulfilment of PAYG unfunded obligations. Following Rizzo (1989), to investigate such an issue Baumol's Law[1] will be recalled and suitably adapted to the unfunded obligation case.

Let us assume that the population is composed only of two generations : workers (L) and retirees (R). During each time period the labour force increases at the rate g

44

and those who were working in the previous period all retire, i.e. each period the retirees are just equal to the labour force of the previous period.

Therefore, in time t,

$$L_t = L_0 (1 + g)^t \qquad \text{where: } L > 0$$

$$g > 0$$

$$R_t = L_0 (1 + g)^{t-1} \qquad t > 0$$

and the ratio between retirees and workers is given by:

$$R_t/L_t = 1/(1 + g). \tag{1}$$

Then, as long as the labour force increases at a steady rate, the ratio of retirees to workers is also constant.

Given a certain labour force L, output is given by:

$$Y_t = \alpha L_t \quad \text{with} \quad \alpha > 0 \tag{2}$$

or

$$Y_t = w_L L_t$$

where α is the average product of labour and w_L is the wage per capita[2]. Given that in this simple model capital does not exist, the product of labour is assumed to be equal to the wage. Changes in productivity are represented by changes in the wage per capita.

The output is assumed to be distributed only between retirees and workers, so that:

$$Y_t = P_t + w_L (1 - c) L_t \tag{3}$$

where P is the amount of pensions paid to retirees and c is the contribution rate. In a PAYG system, pensions are paid out of wages and various formulas for determining pensions might be envisaged. According to the most common arrangements[3] pension entitlements assume the following simple form: the retirees are entitled to receive a given fraction of their earnings in the form of pension benefits, i.e.:

$$P_t = \beta w_R R_t \quad \text{with} \quad 0 < \beta < 1$$

where β is the replacement rate.

Then, (3) becomes:

$$Y_t = \beta w_R R_t + (1 - c) w_L L_t \tag{4}$$

or

$$Y_t = P_t + W_t$$

With the replacement rate thus fixed, if the PAYG budget has to be balanced, so that:

$$\beta w_R R_t = c w_L L_t$$

the contribution rate must be adjusted accordingly. Rearranging and transposing c to the left-hand side:

$$c = \beta\sigma \; 1/(1 + g) \tag{5}$$

where

$$\sigma = w_R / w_L$$

Expression (5) gives us the basic relationship existing between the contribution rate, the replacement rate, the population growth and the productivity growth. Productivity growth is defined as a situation where the wage rate of the working population exceeds the past wage rate of retirees, i.e. where $w_R/w_L < 1$ and population growth as one where the ratio of workers to retirees rises, i.e. where $g > 0$. This relationship can be investigated using simple comparative static results.

If we take the first and the second derivative of expression (5) with respect to g and the partial cross derivative with respect to β and σ, we get:

$$\delta c/\delta x = \beta\sigma/x^2 < 0 \quad \text{where} \quad x = (1 + g) \tag{6}$$

$$\delta^2 c/\delta x^2 = 2\beta\sigma x/x^4 > 0 \tag{7}$$

$$\delta c/\delta x\delta\beta = \sigma x^2/x^4 < 0 \tag{8}$$

$$\delta c/\delta x\delta\sigma = \beta x^2/x^4 < 0. \tag{9}$$

The relationship between the contribution rate and the growth of population can be represented by a decreasing and convex function (fig. 4.1). Different curves allow for different replacement rates (or different productivity rates): the higher the values of β (or of σ) the steeper the cg function becomes. In other words, given a constant population growth, the higher the replacement rate (or the lower the productivity growth) the higher the contribution rate required to keep the PAYG budget balanced.

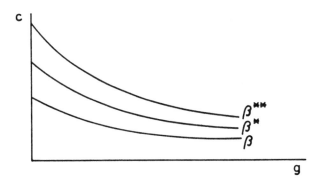

Fig. 4.1. Effects of a change in the replacement rate (or in the productivity growth) on the contribution rate for any level of the population growth rate.

4.2.2 Given the above mentioned relation between the contribution rate, the replacement rate and the rate of growth of population and productivity, the issue to be investigated is the impact of such a relation on the fulfilment of social security unfunded obligations.

The fulfilment of the obligation can be defined in several ways. Let us maintain, in line with most of the existing social security systems, that social security obligations are fulfilled, when β, the replacement rate, is kept constant i.e., $\beta = \bar{\beta}$. Recalling that the PAYG budget is balanced, when

$$\beta w_R R_t = c w_L L_t$$

and therefore:

$$c/\beta = 1/(1 + g)\,\sigma$$

the fulfilment condition implies that as g decreases c has to increase, unless the increase in productivity (i.e. the decrease in σ) is such that the decrease in g is counterbalanced. In aggregate terms, confronting the distribution between the two sectors;

$$P_t/W_t = (\bar{\beta}\,w_R R_t)\,/\,[(1 - c)\,w_L L_t] = [\bar{\beta}\sigma/(1 - c)]\,[1/(1 + g)] \tag{10}$$

or

$$\bar{\beta} = [(1 - c)/\sigma]\,(1 + g)\,(P_t/W_t)$$

as g decreases and c increases (in order to maintain the balance of the PAYG budget) the fulfilment of $\bar{\beta}$ implies that the ratio P_t / W_t has to increase. This means that a larger share of national output has to be transferred from the working sector to the inactive sector of the population. Again, the counterbalancing impact of increasing productivity might reduce such an effect. In other words, if we assume constant productivity, the social security burden has to increase through time because of the "unbalanced" growth of population. In fact,

$$c w_L L_t / Y_t = \bar{\beta} w_R R_t\,/\,[\bar{\beta} w_R R_t + L_t w_L\,(1 - c)] \tag{11}$$

where

$$c w_L L_t / Y_t$$

is the average social security burden. Since

$$\beta w_R R_t / L_t w_L\,(1 - c)$$

increases as g decreases, because of (10), it follows that

$$[\beta w_R R_t / \beta w_R R_t + w_L(1 - c)\,L_t]$$

increases as g decreases, if β is kept constant, and, therefore, the average tax burden increases as g decreases. Therefore, the more unbalanced the ratio of pensioners to workers, the more resources have to be transferred to pensioners for any level of $\bar{\beta}$. Thus,analogies seem to exist with the conclusions of Baumol's Law. On the other hand, if productivity increases, the unbalance in the ratio of pensioners to workers might exert a less severe impact on the PAYG budget. Notwithstanding the relevance of such an argument, the uncertainty of the productivity prospects in most countries (also related to the expansion of labour-intensive services) would suggest not to rely very much upon this factor as a solution to the viability of the PAYG system. Nor it should be overlooked the fact that if unemployment is realistically introduced into the model, the unbalance in the ratio of pensioners to workers is due to increase. Of course, the "net" effect of these opposite forces is a matter of empirical investigation and the highly simplified assumptions underlying the model do not allow general conclusions to be drawn. What is important to stress is that Baumol's Law seems applicable to the case under study and that, therefore, the issue of the fulfilment of PAYG unfunded obligations is worth exploring further.

Two interesting lines of enquiry are suggested by this first conclusion. Firstly, one might ask which value of β will be chosen within the system and whether it is likely to be maintained through time. Secondly, the question arises whether Baumol's Law occurs with any form of fulfilment or whether it is possible to devise a fulfilment formula which avoids the continuous increase of the social security burden for workers, under unfavourable demographic conditions.

4.2.3 Looking at the first issue, let us assume that individuals can choose the level of $\bar{\beta}$. Such a choice can be investigated using a simple life-cycle model because analogies do exist with respect to the choice between present and future consumption[4]. The individual budget constraint, in this case, is given by:

$$w = \bar{\beta} w \left[1/(1 + g) \right] + w(1 - c).$$

Let $\bar{\beta} w = p$; g can be considered as the rate of return on pensions and the expression $1/(1 + g)$ reflects the "price" of pensions. The individual has to choose between pension benefits and present net wage. The behaviour of the model can be analysed in terms of substitution effects. More precisely, any decrease in g will imply an increase in the "price" of pension and, therefore, the slope of the budget line will change and the line will become steeper.

The initial equilibrium changes and the crucial question to be answered is whether the new equilibrium allows for $\bar{\beta}$. The predictions coming from the conventional theory on savings decisions do not entirely apply here. Usually, the issue of the savings decision is analysed in terms of wealth and substitution effects and no unambiguous answer can be given to the question whether saving increases or decreases with the rate of return. The net effect is ambiguous and depends on the relative magnitude of the elasticity of substitution and the wealth elasticity of

48

consumption[5]. In the case of pensions no relevant wealth effects seem to occur given that a decrease in g does not affect the individual's present value of wealth and, therefore, his present consumption.

Diagrammatically, the problem is described in figure 4.2.

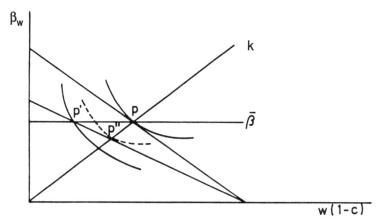

Fig. 4.2. Effects of a fall in the rate of population growth on allocation of resources between future pension and present net wages in the presence of alternative systems of fulfilment.

Starting with an equilibrium P, along the $\bar{\beta}$ line, when g decreases (and c increases) the budget line is shifted because p has become more "expensive" as a consequence of an increase in its price (or a decrease in its rate of return). In order to maintain $\bar{\beta}$, a disequilibrium arises, leading to P'. In this case, the substitution effect is not likely to be counterbalanced by any wealth effect (leading to a reduction in the allocation of resources at the present consumption); theoretically, therefore, a new equilibrium is unlikely to be found on the line $\bar{\beta}$. In fact, even if the degree of substitution between p and w seems to be low, still under conventional forms of utility functions, $\bar{\beta}$ is unlikely to be maintained because it would imply a sharp increase of the contribution rate and, therefore, a reduction in present consumption. Therefore, this leads to the conclusion that, as long as individuals are allowed to choose the allocation of their resources between pensions and present consumption, in the presence of unfavourable rates of population growth (reducing the rate of return of pensions), they are unlikely to support the fulfilment of such an obligation.

Assuming a demand-oriented collective decision-making process, the conclusion that the fulfilment of pensions obligation is an unlikely political outcome implies some strong assumptions which are not necessarily realistic, such as the assumption that, regardless of their age, all the individuals have the same preferences with respect to pensions. However, given such an assumption[6], the result is that if contribution rates were chosen time after time, in the presence of decreasing rates of population growth, the fulfilment of obligation would not be guaranteed because it would not be likely to reflect individuals' preferences. Nor such an argument adequately stresses the fact that individual choices in the pension case might be more complex than those usually assumed by the conventional utility maximizing models[7].

4.2.4 Let us consider the former issue, which has some interesting policy implications. The core of the problem is whether an increasing pensions/wages ratio is inevitable or whether it depends on the institutional features of the social security systems. It follows that alternative forms of fulfilment have to be investigated. As Musgrave (1981) points out, the ideal form of fulfilment should be able to share the "demographic risk", deriving from a declining population growth, between pensioners and workers. A system where retirees receive a constant replacement rate imposes a severe risk on the working population. On the other hand, a system based on a fixed contribution rate places the entire "demographic risk" on retirees. Therefore, in the presence of a declining population both systems contain an in-built potential for collapse.

One possible solution to such a problem might be to maintain the ratio of per capita pension to per capita wages (net of social security contributions) constant[8].

Recalling expression (4), this condition can be expressed as follows[9]:

$$(P_t/R_t) \, / \, (W_t/L_t) = k = \beta/(1 - c). \tag{12}$$

The choice of such a k ratio would be a political matter: once it is chosen, the contribution rate should be adjusted (let us say every five years) to maintain the contractual ratio and it would depend on the number of retirees, of workers and on the fixed position chosen.

An expression for c can be derived from (12): rearranging, and recalling (5) it yields:

$$c = k/(1 + g + k). \tag{13}$$

If the rate of population growth decreases the contribution rate rises but by less than in the previous case, because in this case the burden is shared between workers and retirees. In fact, from (13) it follows that any increase in the number of pensioners with respect to the entire population is reflected on c only for a share equal to k; the remaining burden is borne by retirees, in terms of a decreasing β. In other words, the negative effects of an "unbalanced" population growth on workers would be lessened[10].

k being a less "unbalanced" form of fulfilment than the above described $\bar{\beta}$, let us consider what implications are likely to follow in terms of individual choice, when unfavourable demographic trends occur. Diagrammatically, the problem can be described by adding the k line to figure 4.2. As can be seen, under conventional forms of utility functions, unlikely the $\bar{\beta}$ case, k implies a feasible equilibrium, located in P'' (and a welfare improvement with respect to P')[11]. However, to arrive at any conclusion on this issue, further developments are needed. More precisely, an investigation should be carried out into the relative position of pensions and present net wages in the individual utility function and into the perception of individuals of different ages of pension and present income. The only tentative conclusion stemming from the above analysis is that age matters when decisions on pensions are to be taken[12].

4.2.5 Another relevant qualification to the above model has to be stressed. More precisely, the argument points to the potential instability of a PAYG system, when subjected to exogenous factors: however, it does not adequately stress the fact that individuals' reactions to such exogenous changes are only likely to exhibit certain analogies with conventional utility maximising models. In fact, when dealing with unfunded obligations, the individual choice does not take place in an empty context like the consumption/saving decision, but is part of an ongoing inter-generational relationship. It is unrealistic, and somehow misleading, to assume that the individual choice is not affected by such a circumstance. Moreover, individuals cannot choose, on a strictly personal basis, whether to fulfil the obligation or not, because the payment of social security contributions is compulsory; therefore, the behaviour of the group, more than the individual's behaviour, is worth examining.

Indeed, individuals might reject the obligation when considered collectively, acting as a group (i.e. a generation). In a demand-oriented political decision-making process, where a self-utility maximiser government is willing to satisfy the majority of voters' preferences, the young generation can express its preferences in favour of or against social security obligations through political participation (and accept or reject its fulfilment).

On the other hand, each generation is part of a continuum and the effects of this membership on his behaviour and preferences cannot be disregarded. Unfunded obligations, being a form of implicit debt, cannot be considered only as a type of financial investment which is rejected when not convenient. In chapter 2 it was argued that government is liable for the fulfilment of the obligation and that it is, indeed, the debtor. But government attitudes are affected by voters' preferences[13] and, therefore, to investigate the fulfilment issue means to investigate how the young generation is likely to vote for pensions.

As it has been already pointed out, the lack of temporal coincidence between costs and benefits is the major feature of the pension contract. Under these circumstances, it is pertinent to ask why young people should be willing to join the pension contract, given that they cannot be sure that future social security obligations will be enforced. Indeed, the reason why young people should be willing to vote for pensions has to be explored more carefully.

To address this issue, some further behavioural assumptions are worth mentioning. Usually, the pension system is assumed, to enter the individual utility function in a lifetime perspective and to be evaluated according to its rate of return. According to this logic, if the worker becomes aware that the system is not able to provide him with a rate of return at least equal to the real interest rate, he will not be willing to pay for financing the system. Even without questioning the relevance of this approach, it should be stressed that the individual's calculations are likely to be more complicated. As Buchanan (1983) has pointed out, welfare as well as family considerations have to be taken into account. Even assuming the weakest form of the interdependence of utility function, it cannot be denied that aged must be kept alive. These costs as well as the increased support payments for the members of his family are likely to be taken into account by the worker when deciding whether to contribute to the system or not.

Moreover, the limits imposed by the strict conventional self-utility maximisation paradigm become less strict if other factors – which in reality are likely to affect individual preferences in this matter – are taken into account. Entering the complex and seemingly endless debate on which theory of rational behaviour should be applied to economic decisions[14], is outside the scope of this work. Still, recalling an increasing bulk of economic literature on this issue, some psychological factors, which are likely to bear relevant consequences for the individual decision-making in the pension issue are to be outlined.

Starting from the conventional point of view that "rational" means in line with the demonstrated self-interest of the decision-maker[15], some qualifications are to be added. Individual's decisions might depend to some degree on others. This may involve not only following the example of others in similar circumstance but also behaving in such a way as to please others or gain their approval. Under this latter point of view, the impact exerted by social customs on individual behaviour deserves to be mentioned. A social custom may be obeyed (even though it is to everyone's individual economic disadvantage to obey it) if individuals are sanctioned by loss of reputation for disobeying it (implying high moral costs) (Akerlof, 1980). We might say that reputation as well as social acceptance enters the individual utility function; therefore, actions implying a loss of reputation, although economically convenient, still will not necessarily be undertaken. If this type of argument is explicitly introduced into the case under study, the issue of unfunded obligation fulfilment can be viewed in a new light and the outcome of individual decisions is less predictable.

The above mentioned factors are likely to play a relevant role at a constitutional level i.e. when the "social" contract underlying unfunded obligations is set up and, successively, when it is maintained. This does not necessarily imply that the contract cannot be rearranged, as far as the specific terms of its fulfilment are concerned, when the overall economic and demographic conditions change. Indeed, this might become necessary in order to maintain the fundamental inter-generational redistributive agreement underlying the contract itself[16].

On the grounds of the above considerations, the rejection of the "pension contract" does not seem to have a relevant predictive power; actually, the core of the issue is whether it is possible to devise a formula of fulfilment coherent with the economic and financial soundness of the pension system.

4.3 CONCLUDING REMARKS

4.3.1 To sum up, the simple model presented suggests that in the presence of a decreasing rate of population growth, to keep the replacement rate constant implies the continuous increase of the ratio of pensions to wages through time and a rising social security burden, this effect being mitigated by increasing productivity trends. Some analogies do exist with respect to Baumol's Law. They derive from the fact that the more "unbalanced" the ratio of pensioners to workers is, the more resources have to be transferred to retirees, for any given level of fulfilment. As a consequence, the fulfilment of unfunded obligation might not necessarily be guaranteed through time. However, if more realistic behavioural assumptions are introduced, other than the strict self-utility maximisation paradigm, the rejection of the contract is not necessarily called for, the problem becoming one of structuring the system to make it viable. In the preceding pages, some insights in this direction have been provided.

The highly simplified assumptions underlying the model (for instance,the lack of indexation methods) do not allow general conclusions to be drawn. However, the analysis suggests that there might be interesting lines of enquiry to be explored. Among the others, the public choice implications stemming from this model should be investigated in order to explore how the choices regarding unfunded obligations can be derived from a stylised collective decision-making process. This issue will be dealt with in the next chapter.

NOTES

1. Baumol (1967). As is well known, according to Baumol's Law the opportunities for applying new technologies in governmental service sectors are limited whereas government wages are likely to rise at the same rate as those in manufacturing sectors and, therefore, if the ratio of public to private sectors has to be maintained constant in real terms, increasing resources have to be transferred from the private to the public sector.
2. The wage rate is net of income taxes. Alternatively, since government activity other than social security is not taken into account, we may assume that the only taxes imposed on individuals are social security contributions.
3. Of course, the analogy is presented in a very simplified way, given that in real systems pensions are calculated using more parameters such as number of years of contribution, last period of work earnings, etc., and methods of indexation are used; however, the assumption of a constant replacement rate as a general rule seems to be acceptable.
4. It might be argued that these analogies do hold only to a certain extent because of the features of the inter-generational contract underlying unfunded obligations, which do affect individuals behaviour (further qualifications are introduced in par. 4.2.5). For the time being, however, the assumption that these analogies do hold will be retained. The

fact that the assumptions underlying our model are unrealistic does not necessarily, undermine its theoretical validity: as is well known, widely accepted models in economics are based on the *as if* proposition and there is no reason for refusing the same logic when applied to our social security model.

5. See Atkinson and Stiglitz (1980), P.76.

6. Such an assumption will be relaxed in the next chapter where the relationship between the individual's age and his preferred contribution rate is taken into account.

7. On this issue see 4.2.5.

8. This idea is developed by Musgrave (1981). OECD (1988c) stresses that trends in real per capita benefit levels relative to average real earnings will be a key factor in determining how financing burdens evolve as the age structure of population changes.

9. In expression (12) productivity is assumed as a constant. Such an assumption will maintained in what follows, given that the conclusions stemming from the analysis are not affected by this simplifying assumption.

10. For instance, with respect to the USA system Musgrave (1981) calculates that such a device would reduce the required increase in the tax rate by 0.6 percent (3.9 percent instead of 4.5) and would also imply, a reduction of the replacement of rate of 1.6 per cent, under the assumption of slightly declining population growth.

11. Still, there is no a priori reason to believe that under our restrictive assumptions (all individuals having the same preferences with respect to present and future income) k is likely to be chosen. In fact maintaining k would imply a reduction of present consumption which cannot be justified by the existence of wealth effects (usually characterising saving decisions but not occurring in this case). Therefore, under our restrictive assumptions, even fulfilment, as expressed by k, might not be guaranteed.

12. This issue is further explored in chapters 5 and 7.

13. Different models of government response to voter preferences have been developed in the public choice literature: the median voter theorem and the interest group theory are the most commonly studied and will be discussed, respectively, in chapters 5 and 6.

14. As is well known, the neoclassical assumption of the omniscient self-utility maximiser decision-maker has been criticised and contrasted with other more realistic approaches, taking into account the existing constraints on the individuals' information-processing capacities (on this issue, see par. 3.3.2). Psychological issues are recalled also by Leibenstein (1976) and underlie his concept of *selective rationality*. Rather than maximising, individuals are assumed "to compromise between two sets of opposing psychological forces: the desire to use one's capacities outside the bonds of the constraints inherent in a context and the desire to fulfil the demands of one's superego, that is, the desire to meet as far as possible one's internalised standards, which in part depend on the observed performance of others" (p. 93). The explicit consideration of psychological, anthropological and sociological factors has been seen by Akerloff (1984) as correcting the restrictive assumptions of individualistic maximising behaviour.

15. We are aware that such an approach is not the only one possible; there is a widespread criticism toward the self-utility paradigm because it does not leave room for ethical considerations. This point of view has been recently powerfully restated by Sen (1987). However, confining the analysis to the self-utility paradigm allows for remaining in the same line of thought followed in analysing collective decision-making within the median voter framework (see, chapter 5). Remaining within the self-interest point of view, it is necessary to point out that self-interest should not be considered only from the restrictive perspective of "economic convenience". The interdependence of utility functions allows for the taking into account of a broader view and for the inclusion of redistribution in the individual utility function (see chapter 5). The role of altruism for pension financing is examined by Verbon (1986).

16. Actually, empirical evidence would seem to support this view: as long as no major changes did occur in the demographic and economic scenario (or as long as they compensated for each other) pension systems have grown up, each generation following

the past generation's steps or even assuming more generous attitudes towards retirees. The fulfilment of the contract was established beyond discussion and nobody would have questioned the rightness of the system. This has only recently ceased to be the case, because of the changes which occurred in the demographic patterns of most western countries: as a consequence doubts have been cast upon the survival of the system within its present terms, the subject becoming a matter of economic as well as political concern.

5. Public choice implications of unfunded debt

5.1 INTRODUCTION

5.1.1 In the public choice literature, different models of government's response to voters' demand have been developed. The purpose of this chapter is to discuss the unfunded obligation issue within the public choice framework, using the median voter approach, which is widely considered to be one of the most important developments in this field. Another leading approach, the interest group theory, will be investigated in chapter 6.

This chapter will be devoted to an exploration of the appropriateness of the median voter theorem in explaining the political decision-making process, when unfunded obligations are involved. More precisely, in section 2 the theoretical foundations of this theorem will be reviewed briefly and its theoretical applicability to the unfunded obligations context will be discussed. In section 3, we will investigate what an individual, arbitrarily chosen as a median voter, would vote for, specifying the identity of the median voter within the model. Section 4 will explore how he would choose with respect to present and future consumption. Within the above mentioned simplifications, the problem of choosing the optimal contribution rate will be dealt with in section 5. Lastly, after having pointed out the shortcomings of the model presented in the previous sections, section 6 will be devoted to suggesting lines of investigation and theoretical insights for further developments of the analysis.

5.2 THE MEDIAN VOTER THEOREM AND UNFUNDED OBLIGATIONS

5.2.1 The main purpose of this section is to examine how predictions on the fulfilment of unfunded obligations through the political process can be derived by an application of the median voter hypothesis. The formal model will be developed in the next section: for the time being, our main concern will be to examine how the unfunded obligations issue can be modelled in the median voter framework.

The median voter theorem[1] describes a process of taxpayer choice through the institution of voting, resembling the economic theory of consumer choice through the market, and provides a theoretical link between taxation and expenditure. There exist many models based on this theorem. All of them have in common a central tenet: political competition ensures over time, and under majority rule, the production of a bundle of public services that conforms to the preferences of the median voter. In its simplest form the median voter theorem can be summarised as follows: there is a single political issue to be determined by a simple majority voting rule, through some election process. Each voter is always assumed to vote for his preferred alternative (i.e. there is no abstention) and to be sincere (i.e. he votes according to his preferences and not strategically). The alternatives may all be ranked along a single dimensioned continuum (for example, left and right or the amount of an expenditure) and all voters have single-peaked preferences in this dimension. (For instance, each voter has a most preferred level of expenditure; as expenditure increases or decreases from this ideal level, the voter's level of preference decreases). A voter's ideal point is defined as his most preferred alternative among all the feasible alternatives on the dimension.

Various different models of the election process may be used to arrive at the conclusion that the median voter's ideal point will be the alternative selected by majority rule (the median ideal point being defined as an alternative enabling fewer than one half of the voters to have ideal points below it in the ordering and no more than one half of the voters to have ideal points above it)[2]. Median voter models have been used to investigate a wide range of policy issues. On the other hand, the assumptions underlying these models have been considered to be highly restrictive somehow, their empirical validity has been questioned and further qualifications have been proposed.

A detailed analysis of the different models developed in the literature and tested for within the median voter approach is outside the scope of this paper[3]; therefore, leaving aside their description in the following pages of this section attention will be paid to the application of the theorem to the unfunded obligation case. The arguments developed in the literature for and against the theorem will be recalled when useful to qualify its application to the pension case.

5.2.2 In order to examine how the unfunded obligations issue can be modeled in the median voter framework, we need to identify the median voter. On the grounds of the considerations developed so far, in the case under study there is no reason for identifying the median voter with the median income person, as it is usually claimed in the median voter literature[4]. In fact, there is no reason to believe that there exists any monotonic relationship between income and desired social security contributions (benefits).

A characteristic which seems to acquire relevance is age. Indeed, individual attitudes towards social security are very likely to depend on individuals' age: more precisely, in the presence of uncertainty (regarding the length of life, the likelihood of fulfilment, ...) at any given point in time, the younger the worker the higher is the present value of his "net social security liability" (defined as the estimated difference between the present value of his contributions and future benefits)[5]. On the other hand, retirees, i.e. aged people who are not asked to pay for social security, will be willing to vote for social security contributions (benefits). Therefore, given that the economic calculus is likely to differ for individuals of different ages, the key feature for defining the median voter would seem to be his age. This argument would suggest that the median voter might be found in the median of voting population age distribution[6].

A further question is whether the ideal median point is monotonic with age. This might not necessarily be the case. Other characteristics can influence same aged individuals' preferences. These differences are likely to depend on the particular features of the social security system. For instance, the existence of pension ceilings might imply that social security preferences are not necessarily monotonically related to age; retired individuals who already receive the maximum possible pension will not have any further incentive to vote for increasing contribution rates given that they would not be able to derive any additional benefit. At the same time, people differently endowed with wealth and having sources of income other than earnings are likely to exhibit different attitudes toward social security. No clear-cut conclusion can be drawn on this intra-generational conflicts issue given that the occurrence of these conflicts mainly depends on the features of the social security system[7].

Being aware of the above mentioned *caveat*, we would still support the hypothesis that the median voter for unfunded social security obligations is to be found in the median age individual. In fact, that *caveat* refers to specific features of social security systems which do not always occur and do not allow for establishing any permanent relationship between individuals' social security preferences and variables other than age. Therefore, the median voter seems to be identifiable with the median age individual, without resorting to any undue oversimplification.

The identity of the median voter is likely to be affected by exogenous factors such as the extension of franchising to youngsters (e.g. lowering the voting age); in this case the age distribution of the voting population will change and, therefore, the median voter will be younger.

Moreover, in order to assess this identity, a further issue to be investigated is whether there is any evidence that political participation varies according to age (the effect of such a relationship will depend on the age distribution). These last arguments do not call into question the relevance of age in identifying the median voter but only suggest that such an issue requires careful investigation.

Having identified the median voter, some further questions arise in applying the median voter hypothesis to the unfunded obligation case.

5.2.3 As is well known, in general the treatment of redistributive problems within the median voter framework is not straightforward. Before dealing with the inter-generational redistribution involved by the pension case, the more general redistribution issue deserves some comments.

Problems arise from an application of the median voter theorem to redistributive issues because of the unstable nature of such an issue which does not necessarily allow for stable coalitions, unless constraints are imposed on individual choices. The outcome of the political decision-making process when an intra-generational redistributive issue is involved is a matter of theoretical debate. As Mueller (1979) argues, assuming that the median voter is in power, "one might expect that redistribution will be toward the middle of the income distribution". The argument recalls the thesis developed by Tullock (1971) that in a democracy redistribution goes from the tails of income distribution to the centre.

Different alternative scenarios can be proposed. As Culyer (1980, pp. 104-105) points out, the individuals at the extremes of the distribution might be willing to form a coalition. "This would be in the interest of the very rich, for the really poor could by such an arrangement obtain more transfers and, at the same time, by terminating transfers to the middle groups, the rich would also be better off. It would also be to the advantage of the poor, who would receive more under such an arrangement and, hence, be persuaded to leave the dominant coalition. The paradoxical result is, thus, obtained that the poor may recognise that their interests coincide more with those of the very rich than with those nearer to them in income". In this case, therefore, the median voter would no longer be decisive.

To sum up, on purely theoretical grounds it is not possible to make predictions about the direction of fiscal redistribution in a democracy under majority rule, since the strategy of forming coalitions is part of the complex voting process, unless constraints are imposed. The empirical evidence on the subject is inconclusive, too[8].

A lot of work has been done in the field[9] to focus upon the conditions under which majority rule yields a unique and stable equilibrium. Without entering into the details of this vast literature, let us only consider the main results which can throw some light on the issue under study.

A first point to be made is that, in the literature on majority rule and redistribution, restrictions are imposed on the class of tax schedules under consideration; if such a class is unrestricted no element is stable against majority rule but if attention is restricted to the class of linear tax schedules[10], as is usually the case, this will contain a stable element. Furthermore, other constraints are imposed on such a choice. The importance of the disincentive effects of taxation is clearly recognised in the optimal tax theory[11]. Once these constraints are introduced, there is a limit to the size of redistribution and, therefore, to the tax rate level[12].

The final problem examined in the literature is to derive the tax parameters as an outcome of a decision-making process following majority rule. Broadly speaking, we might say that the existence of different abilities, which determines the individual's earnings level, would allow for single-peaked individual preferences over the tax parameters. In turn, single-peaked preferences over the permissible range of tax parameters would seem to suggest that there is a value for the tax rate which is stable against majority rule: i.e. it cannot be defeated by a majority vote in competition with any other permissible tax rate. Given that, in line with Black's (1948) contribution, single-peakedness is sufficient for the existence of a (non-empty) core in a majority voting game, the preferred tax rate is the one chosen by the median ability level individual. Therefore, on the grounds of the above considerations, a median voter's equilibrium can be theoretically reached when intra-generational redistribution is involved, provided that constraints are imposed on individual choices[13]. The first general question is whether the median voter hypothesis is able to deal with an inter-generational redistributive issue such as the unfunded obligations case.

5.2.4 At first sight, taking a simplistic view, it might be argued that no major differences arise when the inter-generational case is dealt with and that the same line of reasoning might be extended to such a case. Once the social security contribution structure is defined so that the PAYG budget is balanced and the usual efficiency considerations are taken into account, the majority voting will ensure a stable outcome, represented by the contribution rate preferred by the median voter[14].

When compared with the intra-generational case, the inter-generational redistribution shows less room for bargaining and for the forming of coalitions. In fact, quite different interests are associated with different ages and, therefore, a coalition of interests between young and old voters, against the median one, is not likely to occur. This depends on the fact that social security contributions are earmarked taxes, usually following a very simple scheme, i.e. a proportional rate on wages and salaries, which would prevent the formation of any common interest between voters at the extremes of the age distribution. In fact, retirement benefits are to be paid, by definition, by all the workers: within the working generation, interests can be diversified according to age differences but the system does not allow young workers to shift the social security burden to the middle aged. It is not the degree of progressivity to be voted(as in the intra-generational redistribution case) but the amount of resources to be transferred to old people.

Nevertheless, some room for bargaining might exist in terms of earnings ceilings (to fix the maximum amount of earnings on which contributions are to be levied), allowances, and so on. In this case the relevant distribution is not the age distribution but the income distribution[15]. This bargaining, however, can affect only marginally the basic foundations of the social security contract,i.e. that workers pay for retirees. In other words, such bargaining is not likely to reduce the decisive relevance of the median voter. Nor does the issue of how the resources are shared among the beneficiaries seem to be controversial: in fact, very old and middle aged retirees do not have conflicting interests, both being entitled[16] to this redistribution, owing to the inter-generational social contract underlying social security.

60

This conclusion, however, tells only part of the story. It rests on the crucial but not necessarily realistic assumption that voters strongly believe that the system agreed today will continue in the future, regardless of the eventual negative effects on the working generation, derived by economic and demographic changes through time. Indeed, the fact that there is a temporal separation between costs and benefits would suggest that the analysis is more articulated and that a "credibility" problem is likely to arise as far as the fulfilment of the obligation is concerned[17].

From this point of view, it might be argued that the nature of constraints which can be imposed on the median voter choice deserves some further comments. In choosing the contribution rate the response of future generations has to be taken into account. This response does not refer solely to the choice between work and leisure but also to the choice between the present system and an alternative social security system. In other words, the median voter, in choosing the preferred contribution rate, should take into account the disincentive effects as well as the eventual future "deception effect" caused by an inflated contribution rate. When the contribution rate has to be voted for, an inter-temporal perspective has to be adopted: the contribution rate which has to be voted today is constrained not only by the necessity of balancing today's budget without discouraging work effort but also by the necessity of balancing tomorrow's budget, when the median voter himself is due to get his pension, without discouraging future generations' coopera-tive behaviour. If the balanced budget constraint is fixed and not flexible, the optimal contribution rate today does not necessarily satisfy the constraints of tomorrow, given that in the meantime changes in demographic and economic conditions might call for a higher contribution rate, if the PAYG budget has to be fulfilled. Indeed, today's median voter cannot disregard the possibility that the future median voter's likely behaviour will affect his own future pension benefits.

As may easily be seen, relevant differences occur between intra-generational and inter-generational cases. In the former, a static situation, given a linear income tax structure, once the disincentive effects are explicitly taken into account, the optimal tax rate can be derived without any further implication. By contrast, in the latter, the contribution rate which is optimal today does not necessarily turn out to be optimal tomorrow: if the balanced budget constraint is fixed, any decrease in the population growth rate as well as any increase in the rate of unemployment requires a corresponding increase in the contribution rate. Because of these circumstances the optimal future and the optimal present contribution rates do not necessarily coincide: the occurrence of exogenous factors may require an increase in the former with respect to the latter, if the PAYG budget has to be balanced. As a result, and in contrast to the static intra-generational case, the median voter has to make a choice through time and to take a long-term perspective. This does not mean that a median voter outcome cannot be reached, but only that further constraints should be introduced and that the relevance of the disincentive effect of an inflated contribution rate should be adequately stressed.

5.2.5 Unlike the conventional median voter models, where the hypothesis of fiscal misperception is ruled out, in the pension issue this kind of problems is likely to arise. The object of perception being the "net social security liability",[18] workers will vote the contribution rate taking into account the difference between the present value of their tax payments and the estimated present value of the benefits they will receive. Workers of different ages will prefer different contribution rates: assuming the same length of retirement, the shorter the period before retirement the higher will be the preferred contribution rate. Indeed, the argument is strictly related to the above idea that the median voter is in the median of the age distribution. Given this framework, the misperception issue exhibits specific features in this case. Recalling the argument expounded in chapter 3, we might say that the aggregate social security cost is likely to be misperceived mainly owing to the asymmetrical way in which contributions are perceived only by workers, who pay for them. This would lead us to conclude that misperception is systematic, but it does not necessarily mean that the voting outcome will differ from the one preferred by the median voter. In fact, once again, age plays a crucial role: it determines the identity of the median voter and, at the same time, affects the voter's perception. Therefore, the relevance of the median voter does not seem to be called into question by the existence of such a systematic misperception.

5.2.6 The application of the median voter model to the pension issue seems to rise less critical questions regarding its theoretical foundation than it is usually the case. The first question to be answered regards single-peakedness. In fact, the theorem rests on the assumption that a majority voting equilibrium does exist, depending crucially on the pattern of preferences and, in particular, on the characteristic of single-peakedness. When this condition fails to hold the voting paradox may arise: there is no majority voting equilibrium and no decision that can win a majority against another option. In this light, the median voter theorem can be viewed as a way of escaping the paradox, imposing a restriction on the range of preferences e.g. the condition of single-peakedness. The question, then, is whether individual choices regarding pensions tend to be of the single-peaked type. The extent of the argument put forward in the literature, e.g. that multi-peakedness is likely to occur in fiscal choices[19], seems to be limited by the specific features of such an issue. The existence of private alternatives is constrained by the fact that to undertake the social security unfunded obligation is compulsory and, therefore, total contracting out is not allowed (unless the system as a whole is destroyed and a major reform does occur)[20]. However, even if the range of choices is restricted, some possibility of contracting out cannot be excluded *a priori*. For instance, in the U.K., it is possible to contract out of the earnings-related component of the state scheme, while membership of the basic component remains compulsory. In such a case, then, private alternatives for social security obligations can exist only above a minimum level: therefore multi-peakedness becomes a threshold problem which does not imply, as a matter of fact, that single-peakedness does not occur. The answer depends on the characteristics of the existing social security systems. The two-dimension issue also deserves some comments. The specific nature of social security unfunded obligations implies that such an issue is not easily tradeable, at least for aged people. Indeed, the range of choice is more restricted than for other expenditure programmes. For retirees, social security benefits are likely to be considered as due up to a certain point (where the actuarial equivalence between contributions and benefits is reached); in any case, the fact that social security benefits accrue only to a specific part of the population implies that for these individuals (aged people) the trade-off between alternative expenditure programmes is unlikely to occur. Other programmes, in fact, would imply less specific benefits and their financing would be borne by all taxpayers (including pensioners themselves). This might not necessarily be the case for young voters; for them, in fact, the trade-off between pensions and other forms of support programmes is more likely to exist, given that these voters are asked to pay for pension schemes as well as for other welfare schemes. For instance, children's education or health care might be traded off against pensions, the benefits of the former accruing in the present while the benefits of the latter were future and uncertain. However, such a trade-off is limited by the fact that pension systems are financed by earmarked taxes and therefore, they can be said to constitute to a certain extent a separate welfare scheme, the benefits and costs of which cannot easily be traded-off against other schemes.

To conclude, multi-peakedness problems may also arise for social security. Their extent does not seem to be such as to discourage the application of the median voter theorem. In some cases they may be even of less importance than in other fiscal choice contexts.

5.2.7 Another common criticism against median voter models, i.e. the argument put forward by Romer and Rosenthal (1979a) that institutional constraints may prevent median voter outcomes[21], seems to have a smaller scope in the pension issue than in other fiscal contexts. In the case of pensions, bureaucrats are likely to play a less relevant role than in the field of local spending to which median voter models are usually applied.

First, the pension issue is not a public service "produced" by bureaucrats and, therefore, the strong power they derive from their monopolistic supplier position does not accrue, even accepting the unlikely existence of powerful bureaucrats *à la Niskanen*.

Moreover, the main argument supporting Romer and Rosenthal's thesis is that the referendum agenda control prevents the median voter from playing a decisive role. In the social security case the existence of an obligation, although unfunded, does not allow for an "all-or-nothing" choice as in some local spending decisions. Even assuming that social security decisions are taken in the context of a direct democracy, the bureaucratic threat cannot be exerted along the lines suggested by Romer and Rosenthal.

5.2.8 Summing up, on the grounds of the above considerations, the application of the median voter theorem to the pension case seems worth considering. The major feature of this inter-generational redistribution decided through a collective decision-making process seems to be the occurrence of disincentive effects more pronounced than in the intra-generational case. Not only is the labour/leisure choice likely to be affected, when inflated contribution rates are voted for; also the future convenience and reliability of the unfunded obligation itself may come under discussion. In other words, the median voter when choosing the contribution rate (or the replacement rate) has to take into account the fact that pension provisions which, apparently, are optimal in the present, might not be equally satisfactory in the future. The occurrence of conditions which are demographically and economically unfavourable might not allow future generations to afford such a burden. Therefore, the median voter's attitudes toward social security are likely to be affected by the uncertainty involved in unfunded obligations, and by his anxiety not to incur the risk of having his entitlement rejected in the future. This issue reveals a somewhat different approach to redistribution as a median voter outcome, in the sense that more caution is required in the present for a long-sighted individual.

On the other hand, the difficulties usually outlined in applying the median voter theorem exist in this case also but do not seem to acquire such importance as to prevent a fruitful application of the theorem.

In the following section a simple analytical median voter model will be built up to deal with some of the issues raised so far.

5.3 UNFUNDED OBLIGATIONS FULFILMENT WITHIN A MEDIAN VOTER FRAMEWORK: A SIMPLE MODEL

5.3.1 Assuming that the level of unfunded obligations has to be voted for, let us investigate such a choice in the median voter framework. For the time being, for simplicity, let us consider how an individual, arbitrarily chosen as the median voter, would decide with respect to the fulfilment of unfunded obligations. In order to make the analysis as simple as possible, recalling the model exposed in chapter 4, let us assume:

- income comes only from wages (w) and pension (p);
- there is no private saving;
- there is only one public output: pensions, defined as $P = \beta w R_t$;
- social security budget is balanced, e.g. $\beta w R_t = c w L_t$ and, therefore, $R_t / L_t = c/\beta = 1/1 + g$;
- β is the replacement rate, c is the contribution rate. Both are between 0 and 1.

Given these assumptions, let us consider what is the optimum contribution rate for a voter, arbitrarily chosen as the median voter.

Assuming that the marginal utility for present and future consumption is the same, the individual maximum can be written as:

$$\text{Max } U_1[w(1-c)] + U_2(\beta w)$$

subject to the constraint of the balanced budget.

Therefore,

$$U_1[w(1-c)] + U_2(\beta w) + \lambda \left(-\frac{1}{1+g} + \frac{c}{\beta} \right) \tag{1}$$

differentiating with respect to c:

$$-w\frac{dU_1}{dZ} + \frac{\lambda}{\beta} = 0 \qquad \text{where} \quad Z = w(1-c)$$

$$\frac{\lambda}{\beta} = w\frac{dU_1}{dZ}$$

differentiating with respect to β:

$$w\frac{dU_2}{dS}\frac{c\lambda}{\beta^2} = 0 \qquad \text{where} \quad S = (\beta w)$$

$$\frac{c\lambda}{\beta^2} = w\frac{dU_2}{dS}$$

The rate of substitution between present and future consumption is given by:

$$-\frac{\dfrac{dU_1}{dZ}}{\dfrac{dU_2}{dS}} = \frac{\dfrac{\lambda}{\beta}}{\dfrac{c\lambda}{\beta^2}} = \frac{\dfrac{1}{\beta}}{\dfrac{c}{\beta^2}} = \frac{\beta}{c} \qquad (\text{i.e.} \quad 1+g) \tag{2}$$

At any given point in time our individual will choose a combination of present and future consumption which is represented by F in figure 5.1.

The question to be answered is: what happens if g changes? For an increase in g he will consider future consumption more convenient and the budget line will be shifted (as is represented by the dotted line). It is difficult to say how the value of c is affected by such a change: it might remain the same given that more resources are available for paying pensions, allowing for a higher β. In this case the income and substitution effect are likely not to counterbalance each other, given that an increase in g does not produce any relevant wealth effect. In the pension case, therefore, the outcome of individual inter-temporal decisions would seem less uncertain than in the more conventional saving decisions because of the absence of wealth effects.

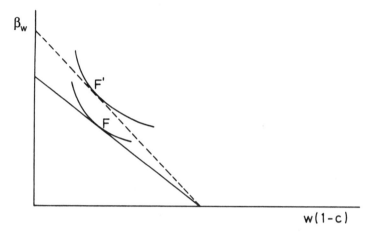

Fig. 5.1. Effects of an increase in the rate of population growth on the allocation of resources between future pension and present net wage (regardless the age of the decision-maker).

5.3.2 The above result was obtained for as if the median voter was fixed. This is not the case; in fact, given the assumptions regarding the population and the crucial role played in this model by g, the very identity of the median voter depends on the rate of population growth g. Intuitively, we can see that if the rate of population growth increases, the median age of the population decreases and therefore, *ceteris paribus*, present consumption will be preferred to future consumption. Thus, any change in g would affect the choice between present and future consumption, because of the induced change in the identity of the deciding voter.

The first step in the development of the analysis along these lines, is to define better the above mentioned intuitive relation between the median age and the rate of population growth, so that any increase (decrease) in g lowers (raises) the median voter age. In other words, the problem is to find a link between population age distribution and g so that we can affirm that the median age is a certain function of g.

This issue has not been explored in the professional literature, probably owing to the strong assumptions needed to arrive at any conclusion. More interest has been concentrated on mean age and its relationship with the growth in population. Let us start by dealing with the effects of population growth on the mean age, following the conclusions reached in the literature. The median age issue will be introduced later.

The problem of establishing a relationship between mean age and the rate of population growth has been approached assuming a stable age distribution[22]. It has been shown that the mean age of a population is related to its rate of increase and that there exists an inverse relationship between the mean age of a population and its rate of growth[23].

Therefore, a growing population tends to be younger than the corresponding stationary population. Moreover, the proportion of people of any age in a stable population can be derived in terms of the rate of increase of the population. It can be shown that in a growing stable population the proportion of the population under any given age is greater than the corresponding one in a stationary population[24].

The problem of establishing a relationship between the median age and such a rate can be developed following the same line of reasoning: how would the proportion of a stable population under the median age, $dC(M)$, change as a consequence of a change in g (in other words, would the median age change)?

$$\frac{dC(M)}{dg} = C(M)\{\bar{a} - a'\} > 0$$

where a' is the mean age of the stable population from age zero to the median age M and $\bar{a}$ is the mean age of the overall population. The above expression shows that the proportion of the population under the median age (or, it is better to say under a given age that, at a certain point in time, is the median) increases as g increases. Given that, by definition, the median age divides the population into two equal sub-groups, if the proportion under the median becomes greater than 50 per cent, to re-establish such equality, the median age of that population has to decrease, as a consequence of a higher value of g.

Transferring this general conclusion to our model[25] it is not unreasonable to conclude that the median voter becomes younger when the rate of growth of population increases.

5.4 THE EFFECTS OF THE POPULATION GROWTH ON THE LEVEL OF UNFUNDED OBLIGATIONS FULFILMENT

5.4.1 Given that the identity of the deciding voter is affected by g and given that his identity, e.g. his age, influences his preferences with respect to future and present income[26], it follows that any change in g affects the median voter choice and, therefore, the outcome of the political process.

Recalling that

$$\frac{dU_2}{dS} = \frac{\lambda}{w} \cdot \frac{c}{\beta^2}$$

and, because of the budget constraint:

$$= \frac{\lambda}{w} \cdot \frac{1}{1+g} \cdot \frac{1}{\beta}$$

$$= \frac{\lambda}{w\beta(1+g)}$$

$$\frac{\delta U_2}{\delta S \delta g} = \frac{-\lambda w\beta}{[w\beta(1+g)]^2} < 0$$

(3)

It means that as g increases (and the median voter becomes younger) the "relative price" of future income increases. This will imply that the median voter will prefer a lower c or a lower β.

There is a difference with respect to the above analysis which deserves to be outlined. When the effects of the population growth on the deciding voter's age were not taken into account, an increase in g was expected to make more resources available for future consumption and to reduce its "relative price", (the decision-maker was assumed to be fixed). On the other hand, if we allow for the effect of g on the identity of the deciding voter, an increase in g, reducing the median voter's age, will affect his preference regarding future and present consumption, in favour of the latter. The slope of the budget line will change and he will prefer a position somewhere on the right of F, for instance F'', (figure 5.2), with a higher level of present consumption. The new equilibrium, therefore, is likely to be found somewhere in the middle between F' and F''; it seems reasonable to locate it on the right of F, because of the relationship existing between g and the identity of the median voter.

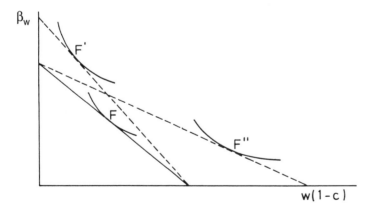

Fig. 5.2. Effects of an increase in the rate of population growth on the allocation of resources between present net wage and future pension. The decision-maker is identified in the median aged individual.

68

5.5 THE CHOICE OF THE MEDIAN VOTER'S OPTIMUM CONTRIBUTION RATE

5.5.1 In the previous section the idea that the younger the median voter is the lower will be his preferred contribution rate has already been introduced. In the following pages it will be developed more explicitly. A simple and stylised model focusing upon the median aged individual will be used. To make the model easy to handle, the analysis will be developed in a static context and no allowance will be made for demographic trends. The effects of these trends on the identity of the median voter will be taken as given, in accordance with the arguments developed in the previous section.

More precisely, we assume that the size of population P is fixed: such a population is composed of individuals who start working at age 0, retire at age R and die at age D. This highly simplified population can be described by figure 5.3

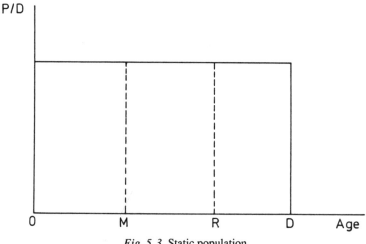

Fig. 5.3. Static population.

Let us consider how a voter of age M, i.e. the median voter, will choose his preferred contribution rate. His utility is a function of his consumption during his working as well as his retirement years. In a very general form[27], it can be expressed by:

$$U_M = (R - M)U_1[w(1 - c)] + (D - R)U_2(A) \tag{4}$$

where:

   A = is the annuity or pension per capita;
   M = median voter age;
   R = retirement age;
   D = death age.

No discount factor is needed under the assumption that the individual does not exhibit preferences for present or future income.

The payment of A is subjected to the constraint that the PAYG budget has to be balanced, i.e.

$$\frac{R \cdot P}{D} wc = (D - R)\frac{P}{D} A \tag{5}$$

From (5) an expression for A can be derived:

$$A = \frac{Rwc}{D - R} \tag{6}$$

Substituting (6) into (4),

$$U_M = (R - M)U_1[(w(1 - c)] + (D - R)U_2\left(\frac{Rwc}{D - R}\right) \tag{7}$$

The median voter desires to maximise the level of his lifetime utility (7) subject to the balanced PAYG budget constraint. Assuming that the retirement age is fixed and unchangeable, the only parameter under his control is the contribution rate. Setting the derivative of the utility with respect to the contribution rate equal to zero:

$$\frac{dU_M}{dc} = (R - M)\frac{dU_1}{dZ}(-w) + (D - R)\frac{dU_2}{dA}\frac{Rw}{D - R} = 0 \tag{8}$$

where:

$$Z = w(1 - c)$$

$$A = \frac{Rwc}{D - R}$$

[Please insert equation here]

From (8) the rate of substitution between present and future consumption for the median voter can be derived:

$$\frac{\frac{dU_2}{dA}}{\frac{dU_1}{dZ}} = 1 - \frac{M}{R} \tag{9}$$

Expression (9) shows how individual M will choose to allocate resources between present and future consumption to maximize his lifetime utility. The higher M is, i.e. the older the deciding voter is, the more resources will be transferred in the future and, therefore, a higher contribution will be voted for[28].

Starting from this simple model it is possible to show that voters' preferences with respect to future and present consumption are affected by age: the older the pivotal voter is, i.e. the greater the median age, the greater will be his preferred future consumption and, therefore, the contribution rate. Taking explicitly into account the relationship between the optimal contribution rate and the median age, the following comparative static results can be obtained from (8).

$$\frac{dc}{dM} = -\frac{\frac{dU_1}{dZ}w}{Rw\left(\frac{d^2U_2}{dA^2}\cdot\frac{dA}{dc}\right) - \left[w(R-M)\left(\frac{d^2U_1}{dZ^2}\cdot\frac{dZ}{dc}\right)\right]} \tag{10}$$

with the intuitive result[29]:

$$\frac{dc}{dM} > 0$$

Because of the simplified assumptions underlying the analysis, the above result is far from being conclusive. However, it seems to give support to the intuitive conclusion that the older the median voter is, the greater his optimal contribution rate is likely to be.

5.5.2 So far the analysis has been based on the unrealistic assumption that the individual utility did depend only on the contribution rate, the other variables being exogenously given. The level of the contribution rate was assumed not to affect the individual incentive to work and, therefore, the amount of resources available for paying pensions. Indeed, the fact that individuals work and that they have to choose not only the optimal contribution rate but also the number of hours to be worked, would suggest that it would be advisable to include in the individual's utility function not only the present disposable income but also the amount of hours of work to be done. Though the relationship between the amount of hours worked and the tax rate is highly controversial[30], allowance should be made for the eventual effects of taxation on work effort. On these grounds, the present disposable income can be written as it follows:

$$Z = w^*[N(c)(1-c)]$$

where:

w^* = wage rate;
N = number of hours worked;
c = contribution rate.

The budget constraint, then. becomes:

$$\int_0^R N(c)f(t)w^*c\,dt = \frac{P}{D}(D-R)A$$

$f(t)$ is the population distribution as a function of age t and, therefore,

$$w^*c\int_0^R N(c)\frac{P}{D}dt = \frac{P}{D}(D-R)A$$

The budget constraint shows that the amount of pensions payable in any period of time depends on the amount of hours worked by young generations, which in turn is a function of the contribution rate.

Given this new budget constraint, (7) becomes[31]:

$$U_M = (R - M)U_1[w^* N(c)(1 - c)] + (D - R)U_2 \left[\frac{w^* c \int_0^R N(c)\, dt}{(D - R)} \right] \quad (11)$$

Taking the derivative of (11) with respect to c, in order to find the optimal contribution rate, we obtain:

$$\frac{dU_M}{dc} = (R - M)\frac{dU_1}{dZ}\left[\frac{dZ}{dN} \cdot \frac{dN}{dc} \cdot w^*(1 - c) + w^* N(c)(-1) \right] +$$

$$+(D - R)\frac{dU_2}{dA} \cdot \left\{ \left(\frac{\frac{dA}{dN} \cdot \frac{dN}{dc} R c w^*}{D - R} \right) + \left[\frac{w^* N(c) R}{D - R} \right] \right\} = 0 \quad (12)$$

where:

$$A = \frac{w^* c \int_0^R N(c)\, dt}{D - R}$$

and

$$Z = [w^* N(c)(1 - c)]$$

In line with the analysis developed in the preceding paragraph, the relationship existing between the optimal contribution rate and the median age can be explicitly taken into account when differentiating (12) with respect to c and M. It follows:

$$\frac{dc}{dM} = -\frac{-\frac{dU_1}{dZ}\left[\frac{dZ}{dN} \cdot \frac{dN}{dc} \cdot w^*(1 - c) + w^* N(c) \cdot (-1) \right]}{(R - M)\frac{d^2 U_1}{dZ^2}\left[\frac{d^2 Z}{dc^2}(-w^*) - w^* \frac{dN}{dc} \right] + w^* \frac{d^2 U_2}{dA^2} \cdot \frac{d^2 A}{dc^2}} \quad (13)$$

The sign of (13) cannot be straightforwardly assessed: it crucially depends on the relationship between the work effort and the contribution rate[32]. Indeed, the specification of the model is such that even the impact of this relationship is not easily identifiable[33]. However, few comments can be made on this issue. It seems significant that, other things being equal, once the amount of hours worked is allowed to vary, the impact of median age on the contribution rate is no longer unique. Such a circumstance would suggest that limits would exist to intergenerational redistribution. In fact, workers might, eventually, respond to high rates reducing the labour supply and, therefore, reducing the amount of resources to be redistributed to pensioners.

Such a conclusion, though highly tentative, would cast some doubts on the idea supported by Browning (1975) and Tullock (1984) that there exist no endogenous limits to the growth of the social security system when an ageing population is required to vote for it. Indeed, *if the PAYG budget is balanced,* at least in principle, these limits are likely to exist, their strength depending on the actual impact of contribution rates on work effort. *Ceteris paribus,* these limits become weaker when the PAYG budget is permitted to become unbalanced and its deficit is covered by external (government) financial intervention. In other words, the growth of the PAYG system might be positively related to the eventual level of its deficit[34]. The policy implications stemming from this argument are that if the growth of the pension system has to be kept under control the PAYG budget should not be allowed to rely heavily upon external financial intervention.

5.6 CONCLUDING REMARKS

5.6.1 In this chapter the relationship between the median age and the optimal social security contribution rate has been investigated. The analysis would suggest that the median age would exert a positive impact on the level of the contribution rate. Such an impact is reduced and become uncertain if the disincentive effects of the level of the contribution rate are taken into account. In other words, an ageing population is likely to favour the growth of the pension system. Such a phenomenon finds its limits in the constraint of the balanced PAYG budget, in the sense that an inflated contribution rate might discourage the work effort and, therefore, impose limits on inter-generational redistribution. Such a conclusion is only tentative and further developments are needed.

The above model, in fact, gives rise to difficulties as far as the modelling of disincentive effects is concerned. The median voter today is likely to be interested not only in the current burden (as a worker/taxpayer in the present) but also in the future burden (as the retiree/beneficiary of the PAYG system in the future). Indeed, the latter aspect might be even more relevant for him, given that an excess future pension burden might discourage future workers from paying social security contributions in the future. Therefore, the issue of the disincentive effects, and its impact on the budget constraint, should be modelled in a dynamic perspective, taking into account:
− the balance of the present period PAYG budget;
− the balance of the next period PAYG budget. The crucial element is the value of g; for low values of g, if the replacement rate has to be kept constant an increase in c might be called for;
− the disincentive effects exerted by the values of the social security contribution required in the future to balance the PAYG budget, for a given level of the replacement rate and of the population growth rate.

Indeed, a contribution rate (and, therefore, a replacement rate), while being optimal in the present for the median voter, might result in incompatibility in the future. The occurrence of unfavourable demographic growth rates might require increasing contribution rates to maintain the same replacement rate.

The above arguments would suggest that given the specific features of the pension issue, modelling the disincentive effects within the lifetime perspective described before might result in an unmanageable analytical construction.

5.6.2 Given these considerations it might be worth exploring alternative ways of modelling the choice of the contribution rate, allowing for the existence of disincentive effects in a static context.

The issue somehow recalls the type of problems analysed within the theoretical framework of the optimal income taxation theory.

No attempt can be made to apply the conclusions reached by those studies straightforwardly to the inter-generational case given that relevant differences do exist between the two fields of analysis. Nevertheless, the optimal tax literature can help to highlight the nature of the problem under review.

Some relevant features of the pension issue should be highlighted (with respect to the optimal tax theory):
- Unlike the optimal tax literature, the tax structure we deal with is a proportional tax structure, where marginal and average tax rate coincide[35]; it implies that the trade-off between equity and efficiency is less severe given that deadweight losses associated with proportional income taxes are usually considered to be lower than those associated with progressive taxes[36].
- Given that our main concern is not the intra-generational redistributive issue[37], no distinction should be introduced between workers on the basis of their different abilities, nor, therefore, on the basis of their earnings. The redistribution issue might be dealt with in relation to two groups of individuals: workers with a given ability who, therefore, enjoy a given level of earnings and retirees who do not work and, who, therefore, do not earn income.
- Our analysis differs from the optimal tax literature, in that the size of the two hypothetical groups of which society is composed, plays a crucial role. It is the changing ratio between these two groups (as expressed by a changing population growth rate) which might imply, *ceteris paribus,* a change in the size of redistribution.

To sum up, far from being conclusive, the argument put forward in this chapter, i.e. that the continuous expansion of a balanced PAYG system is not the necessary outcome of the collective decision-making process in the presence of an ageing population, seems worth considering. Further developments are needed and some lines of investigation have been indicated.

Appendix *

The age distribution of a stable population is given by

$$c(a) = be^{-ra}p(a)$$

where b is the birth rate, r the annual rate of increase and $p(a)$ the proportion surviving from birth to age a, given the mortality schedule $\mu(a)$. The relation of $p(a)$ to $\mu(a)$ is given by

$$p(a) = e^{-\int_0^a \mu(x)\,dx}$$

r and $p(a)$ are all that is needed to determine the proportion at every age in the stable population, since

$$c(a) = be^{-ra}p(a)$$

and

$$b = \frac{1}{\int_0^w e^{-ra}p(a)\,da}$$

If r is zero, the exponential is a constant and the age distribution is the same as the life-table [i.e. a deterministic model of mortality and survivorship].

If $p(a)$ is kept constant, alternative values of r determine different slopes of the age distribution, as is shown in figure 5.4. Higher values of r create stable age distributions that taper more rapidly with age. This tapering effect can be expressed by calculating the relative slope of the age distribution

$$\frac{1}{c(a)}\frac{dc(a)}{da} = -[\mu(a) + r]$$

The relative slope at age a is, with sign reversed, the sum of r and age-specific mortality at a: hence, a stable population with a higher rate of increase but the same mortality schedule has the same increment to its relative slope at every age when compared to the slower growing population. Therefore, the faster growing stable population has a higher proportion at every age up to the point of intersection and a lower proportion above this age.

If the difference in r of two stable populations is very small the point of

---

* This analysis follows Coale (1972).

intersection is the mean age $\bar{a}$ of the stable populations; i.e. both have the same proportion at $\bar{a}$. On the other hand, a faster growing population has a relatively higher $C(a)$ at ages below $\bar{a}$ and a relatively lower $C(a)$ at ages above $\bar{a}$ (both in proportion to the distance from $\bar{a}$).

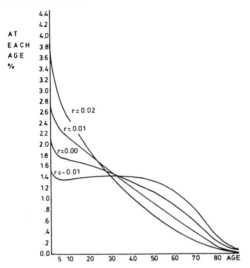

Fig. 5.4. Age distribution of stable populations, showing identical mortality rate and different rates of increase.

This relation between stable age distributions and different growth rates has been described as a "pivoting" action on the mean age. The stable population with a higher rate of increase has a lower mean age.

Since a stable population with a higher rate of increase and a given mortality schedule has a higher relative slope at every age than one with a lower rate of increase, it follows that the proportion under any specified age is greater.

In fact, if $C(a)$ is the proportion under age a in the stable population, it has been shown that:

$$\frac{dC(a)}{dr} = C(a)\{\bar{a} - a'\} > 0$$

where a' is the mean age of the stable population from age 0 to age a and $\bar{a}$ is the mean age of the overall population. Since a' is always less than $\bar{a}$ (until $a = w$, i.e. the highest age attained in the population) $dC(a)/dr$ is positive at all ages.

NOTES

1. It seems preferable to use the word theorem rather than model to refer to the basic hypothesis that under certain assumptions the median voter is the pivotal voter. The same principle, in fact, has been modelled in many different ways and, therefore, it is not easy to refer to *the* median voter model.

2. The median voter equilibrium does not necessarily imply the efficient allocation of resources. As is well known, resources are efficiently allocated when the sum of the marginal valuations of all individuals for the public good equals the sum of the marginal tax prices. The median voter equilibrium only requires that the median voter's marginal tax price equals his marginal evaluation. A sufficient condition for satisfying efficiency would be that tax prices and marginal valuations have the same distribution across the population and that the median taxpayer is the median demander (see, Holcombe, 1977).

3. A careful examination of the results obtained in positive theory is developed in Romer and Rosenthal (1979b) and Marenzi (1987).

4. A proxy for the median voter in fiscal choices is usually found in the median income voter. In the presence of identical tastes, uniform participation in voting and a monotonic relationship between income and desired public spending, the median voter can be indeed, identified in the person of median income. However, this is not always the case. The identity of the median voter may differ with the issue and, furthermore, on any one issue the median voter may not be the one with median income. Other specific characteristics may become relevant for specific expenditures. For instance, dealing with school expenditure, the median voter might be better defined in terms of the number of school children in the family rather than in terms of median income. Therefore, if there are differences in tastes and if the quantity demanded is not a monotonic function of income, the median voter cannot be easily identified merely by considering the median income. The issue becomes even more complex if one allows for the impact of differential voting. As Atkinson and Stiglitz (1980) point out, since voters' participation and eligibility are correlated with income, for a positively skewed income distribution majority voting may tend to reflect the mean, rather than the median income individual's preferences.

5. This concept has been explored in chapter 3.

6. If individuals of the same age have identical preferences, the median voter result, if it occurs, would be efficient (see note 2).

7. An appropriate theoretical framework to deal with such an issue is the interest group approach; its applications to the unfunded social security obligations will be analysed in chapter 6.

8. This conclusion is reached by Pommerehne (1980) in reviewing the existing literature.

9. On this issue, see, Romer (1975).

10. As is well known, linear tax is the simplest form of progressive tax where a guaranteed minimum income is combined with a proportional tax on all income.

11. The efficiency considerations are usually taken into account assuming a revenue constraint on the side of government and the existence of a trade-off labour/leisure on the side of individuals. Individuals are assumed to be differently endowed as far as ability (i.e. human capital) is concerned and their earnings are usually assumed to depend on ability.

12. Such a limit is recognised as being in the interest of the beneficiaries, too. In fact, over-high tax rates, reducing the incentive to work, would lower earned income and, therefore, tax revenue. As a consequence, less income would be available for redistribution. The strength of this argument, of course, depends on the elasticity of the labour supply and on the extent of the effects of taxation on work incentives. This issue is controversial; for a survey of the different positions, see Atkinson and Stiglitz (1980).

13. Before leaving this issue, however, it seems worth pointing out that the median voter equilibrium described above lies within an approach to redistribution, mainly based on "coercion", i.e. it is assumed that in a democracy individuals will use the majority rule to achieve benefits for themselves at the costs of the other members of the society. Indeed, this is not the only approach to redistribution. In literature other models have been offered to explain redistributive activity; these models assume that the observed redistribution from the rich to the poor is effected voluntarily. Two basic explanations are usually put forward (see Rodgers, 1974) to describe why an individual, behaving

rationally, would use a part of his income to improve other people's situation:
- the interdependence existing between the individual's utility functions (altruism,etc..);
- the failure of private insurance to deal with certain risks.

Attempts to explain fiscal redistribution as voluntary assume that all members of the society, participating in the political process, join a social contract and agree on the institutions to be used for carrying out the redistribution. A further assumption is that to carry out a publicly financed income redistribution all the participants are uncertain about their future position. In Rawlsian terms, we might say that men, labouring behind a "veil of ignorance", not knowing the roles they would occupy in society, would willingly consent to income redistribution. These conditions are criticised on the grounds that it is highly unlikely that a generalised state of uncertainty occurs: once we allow for individuals having different future income perspectives, there is no reason to believe that those who expect a superior position in the future will agree on a social contract which is damaging to them in the future.

14. According to Browning (1975) and Tullock (1984), the major feature of such an outcome is that social security transfer will be too large and, therefore, an over-expansion of the system is likely to occur. This issue is addressed to in section 5.

15. A relationship exists between the two distributions: young workers are likely to earn less than older ones but such a relationship does not seem to affect in any systematic way the problem under study.

16. The fact that retirees are entitled to receive the pension introduces a somehow different scenario with respect to the intra-generational case, where recipients cannot claim any "right" to the transfers. Therefore, in this case individuals can be assumed to join a social contract just because they are aware of their future position; i.e. of the fact that they will be aged, and, therefore, recipients of benefit in the future. The fact that social security transfers originate in an obligation gives the individuals the certainty of their future positions (i.e. of being recipients) unless a major change occurs and the system is destroyed (see chapter 4). However, there is no certainty about the exact amount of the transfers they will receive. Therefore, the major claim against the theoretical validity of the voluntary approach (see note 13) does not seem to hold in the inter-generational case. Individuals either because they are risk averse or because they care about aged people's welfare (the fact that social security payments are a substitute for family support might be relevant) will be encouraged to join the social contract (this issue is addressed in chapter 4). However, this does not mean that coercion does not exist at all. We might say that social security is an example of how a *voluntary* redistribution from young to old people can be made on a *large scale*. We are still at a constitutional level; at a post-constitutional level, the uncertainty regarding the mode of fulfilment will lead individuals to make coalitions in order to make the terms of fulfilment as favourable as possible to themselves. It is at this latter stage that coercion is likely to arise.

17. This issue has been explored under a different perspective, in chapter 4.

18. The perception issue has been examined in chapter 3.

19. For instance, taking education as an example, Atkinson and Stiglitz (1980) show that the existence of private alternatives to public education may give rise to multi-peakedness: (for instance, for levels of public expenditure below a certain threshold, individuals may choose private provision whereas for expenditure above that level public provision is preferred). Moreover, as Brown and Jackson (1986) point out, when a two-dimension issue has to be voted on, single-peaked preferences cannot automatically be assumed to exist. For example, if voters are asked to vote for combinations of two different policies no presumption of single-peakedness can be derived from the preference function of the individual voter. Since there is no obvious ordering, the result will depend on how the issues are combined. Only if tastes are highly homogenous there will be an ordering for which all preference rankings are single-peaked. This remark is important given that fiscal decisions are likely to involve many dimensions (multiple expenditure programmes, different parameters of the tax systems).

20. The difficulties relating to such a major change are examined in chapter 4, par. 4.2.5.

21. As is well known, Romer and Rosenthal (1979a) point out that the models strictly based on the median voter hypothesis disregard the impact exerted on the voting outcome by institutional factors. The relevance of these factors has been stressed by Pommehrene and Schneider (1978) too. The conclusion is that systematic differences in spending exist between the direct and representative democracies: *ceteris paribus*, the latter are found to spend more than the former. Institutional considerations have been explored more in depth, as a contrasting hypothesis to the median voter one, by Romer and Rosenthal (1979b). They claim that the institutional structures of political resource allocation may work against median voter outcomes; as long as the referendum agenda control exists and the bureaucratic monopoly power over the alternative expenditures available to the political decision-makers is strong, the expenditure outcome will not coincide with the median ideal outcome. The reason is that the voter can be threatened, being compelled to face an "all-or-nothing" choice. Others (Bennet and Di Lorenzo, 1984) have explored how political competition may be restrained by the operation of political machines, by the ability of politicians to control the agenda presented to the electorate, by bureaucratic influence over public expenditure programmes and by the practice of conducting many public sector activities through off-budget enterprises which are beyond the control and scrutiny of the citizen/taxpayer. These arguments cast some doubts on the predictive power of the median voter models.

22. A stable age distribution exists when age-specific birth and death rates have been constant over a considerable past period (see, Keyfitz, 1977). A *stable population* is characterised by a fixed age composition, constant birth and death rate and a constant rate of increase. The special case of a stable population with zero growth is called the *stationary population*. The stable population model is usually used to provide answers to questions concerned with the behaviour of population's parameters, such as, for instance, age.

23. For more details, see the Appendix at the end of this chapter.

24. This line of reasoning is described in the Appendix at the end of this chapter.

25. In our model, population is described in a very simple way, adopting a geometric growth hypothesis. However, this simplification does not seem to alter the conclusion that the median age decreases as the rate of population growth increases.

26. The influence of age on the median voter's preferences between present and future consumption becomes more evident if the problem is stated in terms of median voter's lifetime consumption, as it follows:

$$U_M = \int_0^R w(1-c)\,e^{-rt}\,dt + \int_R^D c(1+g)w\,e^{-rt}\,dt$$

where r = rate of interest and D = death date.

The shorter the length of time between M and R, i.e. the older the median voter (assuming R as fixed), and the greater the utility deriving from an increasing contribution rate.

27. In expression (4) the death date is considered to be fixed. Two simplifying assumptions are required. Firstly, the specific death rate is assumed constant, regardless the age. As Keifitz (1977) argues, such a simplification is often used for short intervals of age: this seems to be the case in our model given that the median age is reasonably expected to vary only within narrow intervals. Secondly, it implies that the death date is known. Clearly, this is a much stronger assumption. Though it is not realistic, it has been introduced because it allows for avoiding major technical specification problems. Indeed, if the death date had been expressed in terms of the expected length of life, the problems should have been modeled in fairly complicated probabilistic terms.

28. For instance, for $M = R$, (9) is equal to zero, given that the marginal utility of consumption is decreasing, dU_2/DA becomes smaller and smaller in proportion to dU_1/dZ, the greater the amount of resources transferred in the future. On the other hand, taking the other extreme and assuming $M = 0$, i.e. to the lowest age of the population, (9) becomes

equal to 1, i.e. the resources will be equally allocated between present and future consumption. This latter unrealistic result depends on the equally unrealistic assumption that the wage is exogenously given, i.e. it does not depend on the amount of work. This assumption is relaxed in the next paragraph.

29. The denominator of expression (10) is of negative sign. In fact, because of the decreasing marginal utility of consumption, the second derivatives of A and Z are of negative sign and, therefore, both sides of the expression on the denominator are negative (with $R > M$).

30. Workers' reaction against wage taxation is extensively dealt with in the literature (see Brown, 1983 and Hausman, 1985). On purely theoretical grounds no clear cut predictions can be formulated,i.e. work effort increases or decreases as a consequence of taxation. On the other hand, empirical evidence does not provide unambiguous support for either conclusion. Still, the argument is worth exploring, especially given the extensive application it has received in the optimal income taxation literature. It seems important to stress the fact that this type of workers' reaction towards an increasing social security contribution differs from the one discussed in chapter 4, where the workers' generation was assumed to face only two alternatives: to fulfil or to renege the obligation. Indeed, in this case a third alternative is introduced; in fact, reducing work effort can be considered a form of "formal cooperation" while, in practice, the workers generation tries to reduce the pension burden imposed upon him. On the basis of the arguments exposed in chapter 4 the extreme case of total rejection has not been taken into account here.

31. It might be argued that (11) shows a certain inconsistency, given that the only argument of the median voter's utility function is disposable income while the impact of the contribution rate on work effort is explicitly taken into account in the same function. Indeed, N(c) is meant only as a simple means of expressing a wider phenomenon, not easy to be handled otherwise, i.e. the median voter awareness that the fulfilment of the obligation in the presence of aging becomes uncertain.

32. Such a relationship affects the sign of (13) directly and indirectly, because of its effects on d^2U / dZ^2 and d^2A / dc^2.

33. If we express d^2A / dc^2 explicitly:

$$\frac{dA}{dc} = \frac{w*}{D-R}\left[\int_0^R N(c) + c\frac{d\int_0^R N(c)}{dc}\right]$$

$$\frac{d^2A}{dc^2} = \frac{w*}{D-R}\left\{2\left[\frac{d\int_0^R N(c)}{dc}\right] + \frac{cd^2\int_0^R N(c)}{dc^2}\right\}$$

The meaning of the above derivative crucially depends on the relationship existing between N and c. Alternative assumptions can be put forward. If we assume that the number of hours worked varies in the same proportion (with respect to the contribution rate) at the various age, d^2A / dc^2 is equal to zero given that the integral can be considered as a constant. Alternatively, if such an assumption is relaxed, and the impact of taxation on work effort is allowed to vary with age, the sign of d^2A / dc^2 will depend on the relationship between N and C. As a consequence, it cannot be predicted unambiguously (see note 30). Moreover, further qualifications might be introduced, relaxing the assumption that retirement age is fixed and not dependent upon the contribution rate.

34. This question recalls the issue dealt with in chapter 3 on the "non-equivalence" of debt with respect to taxation and its rationale can be derived using the same arguments.

35. Eventually, social security contributions are proportional to earnings with an upper limit, which means that they can be regressive.

36. Recently, on this issue, see Stiglitz (1986).

37. Indeed, relevant intra-generational redistributive issues arise because social security transfers different amounts to aged individuals, according to their different circumstances. Such an issue is outside the scope of this chapter and will be dealt with in chapter 6.

6. The interest group theory and unfunded obligations

6.1 INTRODUCTION

6.1.1 The economic approach to political behaviour assumes that actual political choices are determined by the efforts of individuals and groups to further their own interests. The median voter approach described in chapter 5 emphasises the relevance of voters' preferences as represented by the preferences of the median voter. Individuals seeking to influence the operation of the state are assumed to act individually.

In this chapter, the role played by interest groups will be examined briefly. More precisely, in section 2 a short general overview of the literature on interest groups will be provided, with respect specifically to the role they are assumed to play in the political process. The relevance of interest groups to the pension case and their impact on the political outcome will be explored in section 3. Section 4 will provide some concluding remarks: the conclusions reached in the specific field of social security will be reviewed in the light of the conclusions reached about the interest group theory.

6.2 INTEREST GROUPS AND THE POLITICAL PROCESS

6.2.1 Interest groups have been widely studied and there is much relevant literature in the field of political science, economics and sociology on this issue. Leaving aside any attempt to revise the several contributions on this topic[1], let us outline the role which interest groups are assumed to play in the political process.

The interest group theory of government[2] is based upon the premise that a major portion of government activity is devoted to the transfer of resources among citizens or different sectors of the population. The basic idea is that interest groups play a relevant role in explaining the political decision-making process and affect economic outcomes in significant ways.

It is assumed that individuals belong to particular groups defined by occupation, industry, income, geography, age and other relevant characteristics[3] that are assumed to use political influence to enhance the well-being of their members[4]. Because of the costs related to their activity, it is unlikely that interest groups are formed *ad hoc* to influence government economic decisions but rather that they, existing as they do for different and more general purposes, can be used to obtain fiscal benefits. Being multipurpose, interest groups might be rewarded for the costs incurred in the political market by the membership for the others activities they pursue[5].

It is recognised that different kinds of interest groups exist: economic interest groups (unions, industry and trade associations, professional associations), moral and religious groups. It is recognised that the more exclusive the services provided by a group are the higher their economic value and the more effective the group is in limiting free-riding.

To what extent interest groups are effective in influencing the political outcome is a matter of theoretical debate, the answer depending not only on the group behaviour but also on the way in which it is assumed the collective decision-making process works. Interest group models refer to two main subjects: the analysis of the interest groups' behaviour, within a given institutional setting, and the analysis of how groups form and effect legislative choices, in order to capture rents from government activity.

6.2.2 Without claiming to survey this vast literature, let us merely point out the most relevant developments, for the purpose of linking our analysis to the previous literature. The interest group theory was stated originally in terms of economic regulation, to explain the pattern of regulatory intervention in the economy. The simplest form of this theory is usually stated as a "capture theory" of economic regulation: producers are assumed to be so small in number that the potential gains from lobbying for legislative protection from competition are likely to exceed the costs. Gains for producers come at the expense of consumers/voters. Despite the losses in real income that they bear because of the monopoly-supporting legislation, consumers' interests are assumed to succumb to producers' interests because consumers are a large group facing high organisation costs.

A more general approach to the interest group theory is provided by Stigler's (1971) and Peltzman's (1976) contributions. The former states the interest group theory in terms of the costs and benefits to various groups of using the state to increase their wealth. Stigler essentially puts the interest group theory into a testable form: he shows that it is conceivable, given certain costs and benefits, that some larger producer groups will find it convenient to seek wealth transfers from the state while some small producer groups are more likely to organise in order to resist negative government regulation. Peltzman generalises the theory, suggesting the existence of a voter-maximising regulator who has to trade-off the rents he gives to producers against the costs he imposes on consumers. He demonstrates that regulatory price-setting does not necessarily provide gains for the regulated industry. More recently, Becker (1986) offers empirical support to the Peltzman theory pointing out that public interest can be in some cases protected even when in direct conflict with the interests of a pressure group, the reason being the self-interest of the legislator. In fact, legislators seeking reelection tend to protect those interests which support this result, especially when the public's awareness and voting participation are high. Through these generalisations, the analytical relevance of the interest group theory becomes autonomous from the theory of economic regulation and interest groups are recognised to be part of the political process.

6.2.3 Within the above described scenario interest groups are considered pivotal actors in the political market, their contractual power being the main variable taken into account by politicians. Actually, the political decision-making process, envisaged by such an approach, can be described as follows: there exists political competition and parties attempt to maximise their expected votes to win the elections. According to this approach, to achieve such an aim, instead of competing for individual votes, parties are assumed to compete for interest groups' support. As Mueller and Murrell (1985) point out, competition for interest group support is likely to take place prior to an election. After the election, governing parties bargain with their interest group supporters and carry on the political allocation resulting from the demand of pressure groups[6]. The next election brings a new competition for pressure groups and it is likely that the set of interest groups represented in the government differs from those in the previous one and different expenditures will be sought[7].

In other words, interest groups are assumed to "trade" votes with a given party in exchange for promised favours for their membership[8]. Representatives are chosen by these interest groups on the basis of the value that the group assigns to the particular policy or law in which it is interested, these values being determined by summing and discounting the net benefits of any particular action over those potentially affected. Therefore, political competition is assumed to be based, not on general political platforms but on specific tax and spending devices which are demanded by interest groups.

The favours (or "fiscal rents") interest groups seek to achieve differ. Some of them, for instance, a quote to protect a given industry or, more generally, regulation devices, are costless and do not necessarily have a direct impact on government budgets. Others, like tax allowances or specific spending programmes do affect the size of the budget and involve direct benefits to economically or geographically separate interest groups, the cost of which is borne by the collectivity.

It is likely that in the long-run such a process will affect the level of public spending (when fiscal devices other than costless regulation are demanded). The political competition would induce each party to increase the number of interest groups supporting it (in response to an increase in the number supporting its opponents). Therefore, the number of interest groups in the political market is assumed to be an increasing function of the number of groups already existing and the demand for government spending favouring interest groups is likely to be greater the more interest groups there are. Mueller and Murrell (1985) tested a similar hypothesis and found a consistent positive relationship between the number of interest groups and the size of government[9].

As can be seen from the above, the concept of political participation itself differs from the one underlying the median voter theorem. The idea that the taxpayer choice through the institution of voting resembles the consumer choice through the competitive market does not hold any more. In fact, voters' preferences do not have the same weight, as they would have in a competitive political market; on the contrary, their "weight" will depend on the effectiveness of the group which represents them[10].

6.2.4 As has already been pointed out, interest groups' effectiveness does not depend, exclusively and necessarily, on the number of votes under the groups' control, i.e. on the absolute size of the group, but on its relative position. Indeed, some empirical evidence does exist that politically powerful groups tend to be small in relation to the size of the groups taxed to pay their subsidies[11]. In other words, when the existence of interest groups is taken into account, majorities are not the only fundamental determinants of political influence in democracy. From this conclusion, other major differences with respect to the voting models derive.

As Becker (1983) has recently argued, when interest groups are taken into account the political equilibrium, is not an "all-or-nothing" outcome, as implied by the models of political behaviour where the majority wins and the minority loses. Indeed, losers are likely to be able to limit the political gains of winners. The identity of winners and losers and the amounts won and lost are not rigidly determined by the nature of the political system, whatever it is, because they are also affected by the political activities of each group. Losers need not accept passively their fate but can exert many kinds of political pressure (lobbying, threats, disobedience ...) to raise their influence.

Some features of interest group behaviour are likely to move in this direction. Mainly, the effects of the increasing costs incurred by taxpayers to finance subsidised activities should be taken into account. More precisely, any increase in the burden borne by taxed groups (in terms of higher tax rates, of cost opportunities or of distortions in the use of resources), is likely to stimulate efforts by taxed groups to lower their burden: since the costs of group action are unchanged, such an action becomes more convenient given that it would allow for larger eventual gains. This favourable effect of the political activities of taxed groups gives these groups an "advantage" in influencing the political outcome. Therefore, spending policies characterised by increasing costs are likely to get less support and stronger opposition than other policies, implying lower costs[12].

In summary, from the above it follows that, the interest group theory, unlike the median voter approach, does not allow clear-cut conclusions to be drawn on the outcome of the political process. Indeed, in trying to encompass the complexity of the political market the theory spotlights a very complex picture and it becomes more difficult to predict the political outcome given that its determinants are not simply the median voter's preferences, representing those of 51 per cent of the voters. In the following section the theoretical framework described above will be applied to the unfunded obligation case.

6.3 INTEREST GROUPS AND UNFUNDED OBLIGATIONS

6.3.1 The main purpose of this section is to examine how the unfunded obligations issue fits into the scenario described above.

The first step is the identification of the interest groups which are relevant to the case under study. The relevant (and increasing) share of government budget used for paying pensions, the unavoidable economic, political and ideological implications involved in such an appealing issue would suggest a continuation of a broad analysis including not only old age groups but also the major established interest groups: unions and business organisations[13]. In other words, if we recognise that social security is a matter of economic policy concern it is indubitable that all the major actors in the political market do have general interest in it.

Such a wide perspective will not be followed here. The reason is that labour and business organisations are multipurpose interest groups so that, for them the pension issue is just one of the several issues subject to their political action. Therefore, their position in this field is only part of a wider activity which is strongly affected by political as well as ideological motivations: any analysis of these motivations is outside the scope of this study. At the same time, the key role they play in any country's economic policy implies that their action is affected by the features of the political, economic and social environment (for instance, the characteristics of industrial/labour relations). Again, the analysis of these wide issues goes beyond the scope of this paper. On the other hand, adopting a broad perspective without looking at these features would only lead to vague results.

For the above reasons, business organisations will not enter the picture. The analysis of labour organisations' behaviour will be confined only to some specific aspects. More precisely, ideological as well as social motivations will not be taken into account and only the narrow economic calculus underlying their political participation will be examined. In other words, social security will be considered as any other government regulatory intervention and only the groups who might, strictly speaking, be described as beneficiaries will be taken into account. Workers, being both taxpayers and beneficiaries, although at different points in time, will be included but the analysis will be confined to these specific features.

6.3.2 Not surprisingly, the organisations representing retirees and elderly pressure groups have the most direct interest in defending the social security system. Age, therefore, should be the common basis for the most involved interest groups[14]. The old age interest groups are likely to be strongly committed to the maintenance of the system (or to its improvement), the principal focus being on benefit levels and on coverage. This commitment can be expressed in several ways using all the available means of political participation[15].

Whether demographic trends, in the sense of population ageing, make old age interest groups more influential is controversial. On one hand, the increase of dependency ratios would lead to increased social security contributions and, eventually, to related opportunity costs. On the grounds of the considerations developed above, the likely effect would be an increase of the pressure exerted by taxed workers. On the other hand, in defence, at least, of the existing benefits structure, retirees might react against what is perceived as a menace deriving from the workers' concern for ageing trends and the related negative effects. Effective pressure, improvements in their political organisation and political appeal can overcome the increased resistance of taxed groups.

The analysis becomes more complex if we allow for the fact that the membership of old age benefit groups does not depend solely on age but can be somehow linked to specific categories (civil servants, professionals, farmers, ...). This latter phenomenon is likely to occur when disparities do exist between categories as far as pension "treatment" is concerned. In such a case, old age groups' demand for new privileges (or the maintenance of the existing ones) can be coupled with analogous activities, carried on by unions. Union's participation, however, is much more complex than that. Let us examine how unions evaluate social security obligations fulfilment.

6.3.3 Traditionally, labour movements support social security. Apart from ideological reasons, the pension issue is closely linked with unions' interests. Assured retirement frees jobs for younger members; at the same time, old age benefits may be used as a framework for collective bargaining.

But there are several scenarios that might gradually reduce unions' support for the fulfilment of unfunded obligations (in the sense of maintaining a fixed replacement rate). As has been already pointed out, unfavourable demographic trends could produce conflict between retirees or older workers, convinced that they deserve retirement benefits because of the contributions paid, and younger workers who bitterly resent the increased contributions necessary to maintain the system. The more visible the payroll tax the higher the degree of conflict is likely to be.

However, family ties across generations could modify this inter-generational conflict. Social security, being a substitute for family obligations, may be seen as a desirable device, limiting the responsibilities of younger adults for elderly parents[16]. Given the inter-generational factor, therefore, unions' activity will be affected by the preferences of their members in the sense that the ideological support for the fulfilment has to be weighted taking into account younger workers' preferences.

6.3.4 Moreover conflicts may exist not only between generations, but also within them. For instance, an intra-generational example of contrasting interests depends on the differences in retirement age existing between white collar workers and/or professionals with respect to blue collar workers. Where these differences exist and are marked[17], they might imply greater behavioural discrepancies between different social classes in the older generations. For example, if professionals retire less and later than blue collar workers, they may, even earlier in life, resent payments that seem too high to support the "idleness" of other identifiable groups. Moreover, these categories and, more generally, high income workers are more likely to be covered by private pension schemes and, therefore, to resist any increase in social security taxation.

These kinds of intra-generational conflicts would leave room for the existence of a plurality of specific, narrowly oriented interest groups (or sub-groups). Indeed, the degree of union fractionalisation might be considered an indicator of intra-generational division of interests. Analogously, the fragmentation of intra-generational interests can occur also because of the existence of disparities between different categories of workers as far as pension provisions are concerned. Differences in contribution rates, retirement ages, replacement rates and pension ceilings imply the existence of a *de facto* intra-generational redistribution among various categories[18].

This situation is potentially a reason for the existence of interest groups, with very narrow scopes, basically aimed at exploiting the system to achieve new privileges or to maintain the existing ones. The demand for these privileges does not necessarily depend on age: in fact, any specific category of workers can seek to obtain privileges at the expense of the overall working population and, therefore, even young people may perceive such action as profitable. This does not exclude the possibility that the profitability of such action can increase with age. Because of the existence of these disparities in pension provisions, and also because of differences within the more traditional multipurpose interest groups, such as the unions, there is room for the existence of narrow interest groups, seeking privileges for specific categories[19].

Summing up the complex scenario just depicted would suggest that, as far as inter-generational conflicts are concerned, labour unions are not likely to support the fulfilment of unfunded obligations in terms of a fixed replacement rate, given that younger workers' concerns cannot be neglected. Political pressure for a fair sharing of "demographic risk" is more likely to occur[20]. Furthermore, the existence of an intra-generational fragmentation of interests would suggest a more articulated outcome, with the benefit issue no longer being the central theme of the discussion. The achievement of privileges of various kind is likely to become one of the ends sought by interest groups. In this case, age conflicts do not necessarily arise given that, even for young workers, it is convenient to call for specific privileges, the costs of which are borne by all the workers.

6.4 CONCLUDING REMARKS

6.4.1 From the above considerations no clear-cut conclusions but only tentative suggestions can be drawn. The purpose of this chapter is not to contrast rival theories but to look at a different public choice approach from the median voter one, to ensure that our picture of the collective decision-making process, when unfunded obligations are involved, is not biased by omitting relevant features of this process.

In this specific context, the applicability of the median voter approach cannot be rejected *tout court* when the existence of interest groups is allowed for, but it needs to be qualified. Basically, age would still remain the major factor influencing voters' social security demands. However, some notes of caution have to be introduced. Allowing for the existence of interest groups, political participation becomes more complex than the "one man one vote" model underlying the median voter approach. In fact, different votes have different weights and, therefore, the 51 per cent of voters might not necessarily be able to impose their own preferences. The political decision-making outcome becomes more difficult to predict.

6.4.2 Although no clear-cut conclusions can be drawn, some insights can be derived on the basis of the above considerations. The existence of many potentially different interests, the extent of which depends on the institutional features of social security systems, implies that different demands do exist. Therefore, it follows that several median voter demands for social security legislation also exist. Other things being equal (and in particular the population age structure), the interest groups theory would predict that a larger number of interest groups would imply higher demand for social security provisions. In this scenario, age does not necessarily play a relevant role: intra-generational redistribution is likely to be the major determinant of the demand for social security and factors others than age may be assumed to lead to the group formation.

On the other hand, a different scenario can be depicted. Let us imagine a rather homogeneous social security system which does not allow for the formation of specific interest groups and for marked intra-generational redistribution. In this case, age would be the major factor influencing political participation but, still, the effect of the ageing process on the political outcome (the level of social security contribution rates) is not as straightforward as it was in the median voter context. In this case, in fact, not only the number of voters but also their "weight", or the intensity of their political participation, has to be taken into account. In fact, ageing implies an increase in deadweight costs. As a consequence, taxpayers can be encouraged to react and organise themselves to influence the political decision-making process, in the sense of reducing pension provisions. The result of the competition among these interest groups cannot be unambiguously predicted and is a matter of empirical investigation.

These remarks on the activity of pressure groups in the pension field, though provisional, must suffice for the present. They were not developed merely for the sake of presentation and will be recalled in chapter 7, where an attempt of empirical investigation will be carried out.

NOTES

1. For a survey, see Salisbury (1975).
2. Actually, there is not a proper theory to refer to but several models have been developed on the basic idea that interest groups are relevant actors in the political process.
3. The definitions of the factors underlying the group formation is a matter of theoretical debate. According to the traditional view of interest groups, it was taken for granted that individuals with common interests would tend spontaneously to form groups to further these interests and no distinctions between small and large groups were drawn, at least as far as their capacity to attract members and their effectiveness were concerned. This view is challenged by Olson (1965) who questions whether it is in the interest of individual members to join interest groups providing collective goods. Assuming that individuals are rational, in seeking to explain why interest groups of different size do come into being, the costs and benefits of alternative courses of action are to be taken into account. These costs and benefits are assumed to be related to the group size. More precisely, Olson argues that when large groups provide only collective goods, free-riding arises and individual members would not have any rational incentive voluntarily to join the association; in large groups collective goods can be provided only if organisations are able to make membership compulsory or if they also provide some non-collective goods in order to give potential members an incentive to join. This is not the case for small groups where each member gets a substantial proportion of the total gain and, therefore, a collective good can often be provided by the voluntary, self-interested action of the members.
4. Indeed, some organisations might fail out of ignorance to further their members' interests and others may be aimed at serving only the aims of the leadership. But, as Olson points out, organisations often perish if they do nothing to further the interests of their members. For this reason, the groups which are usually focused upon are expected to further the interests of their members.
5. In the light of his explanation of group formation, Olson suggests that these groups provide, as "by product", services for their members (journals, legal assistance, advising and consulting services) and, hence, use the "profit" on these activities to finance collective action.
6. Government is assumed to satisfy interest groups' preferences. A more general approach to the political market should take into account the political power of suppliers, parties as well as bureaucracies.
7. This does not necessarily mean that expenditure increases. In fact, this new set of interest groups might consider the previous level of government spending excessive and, thus, call for a reduction.
8. This trade-off can take many forms: an interest group may endorse a party, supply campaign volunteers or contribute funds for the party's campaign.

9. Such an hypothesis is tested together with several additional variables deriving from the public choice literature, under the assumption that the impact of these factors is additive. Political participation and population are found respectively to be, positively and negatively related to government size. It is interesting to note that higher percentages of voters in a given population mean higher percentages of low income voters relative to high income voters. (The supposition is that lower income groups tend to be excluded from voting *de facto* if not *de jure*. This supposition is based on empirical evidence). The Meltzer and Richard (1981) hypothesis that greater participation by low income voters leads to more redistribution and greater government size is, thus, supported.

10. As Becker (1983) points out what matters is not the group's absolute efficiency, i.e. its absolute skill at controlling free-riding, but its efficiency relative to the efficiency of other groups. According to him, "the emphasis on the free-riding in many discussions of the effectiveness of pressure groups is a little excessive because political success is determined by relative, not absolute, degree of control over free-riding" (p. 380).

11. To support this argument Becker (1983) refers to the evidence for agriculture in different countries: it is heavily subsidised when it is a relatively small sector (as in the United States or in Japan) while it is heavily taxed where it is a relatively large sector (as in Poland, China or Thailand).

12. Becker (1983) reaches somehow similar conclusions based on different premises in a formalised model on interest group competition. He assumes a budget equation where subsidies do not necessarily equal taxes because of the existence of deadweight costs on both sides of the budget. According to this approach, an increase in the marginal deadweight cost of taxes is considered to raise the pressure exerted by taxpayers, essentially because a reduction in taxes, then, has a smaller adverse effect on the revenue from taxation.

13. In the field of political science Stearns (1982) provides an interesting contribution following these lines with reference to the USA situation.

14. As Browne-Katz and Olson (1983) and Borgatta and McCluskey (1980) point out, in the United States, in recent years, "ageing has been discovered" and several groups concerned with ageing policy have been formed.

15. A peculiar example of this commitment does exist in Italy, where a "pensioners party" was formed in the seventies.

16. Analogous considerations are developed in chapters 3 and 4.

17. Stearns (1981) points out that in the USA a ten year spread does exist between average retirement ages of key occupational groups.

18. In Italy, for instance, civil servants are given a pension after a shorter period of contribution than private industry workers and local government employees. Moreover, civil servants' pension is calculated on a more favourable earnings base than private industry workers' pension. Another interesting example is given by the fact that some categories of workers, for instance farmers, pay very low contributions as compared with the promised benefits and, in practice, are subsidised by other workers. The above examples are only some of the several anomalies characterising the Italian social security systems. For an interesting analysis in this sense, see Castellino (1981; 1984).

19. This situation does not necessarily go in the direction of an increase in the social security budget: in fact, professional or high-income categories of workers, regardless of their age, might seek to contract out from the public system and to rely more on private options.

20. The scenario is much more complicated. So far, an unmodifiable PAYG system has been assumed. However, this is not necessarily the case; changes in the financing system might be called for, in the sense of general revenue financing. Income taxation versus value-added taxation is a matter of theoretical and political debate.

7. An attempt at empirical investigation

7.1.1 The conclusion stemming from chapter 5 is that an ageing population will vote for an increasing social security system, although subject to some constraints. The basic assumption underlying such an hypothesis is that the political outcome reflects the median voter's preferences and, therefore, broadly speaking, that the older the median voter is, the larger will be the security system preferred by him[1]. This effect is likely to be tempered by the disincentive effects of the high contribution rates required to balance the PAYG budget in the presence of an ageing population.

The conclusion that an ageing population will vote for an increase in pension provisions is not new in the literature: Browning (1975) and Tullock (1984) discuss the social security growth issue outside any formal model and arrive at analogous, although clearer-cut conclusions[2]. Yet, surprisingly, little has been done to develop and test for the hypothesis concerning the impact of demographic factors on the political decision-making outcome, at least as far as pension provision is concerned[3].

This chapter is aimed at exploring this issue. The analysis will be enlarged to take into account the further qualifications introduced in chapters 5 and 6, which examined the impact exerted by economic constraints and the role played in the political process by pressure groups, respectively. Moreover, tests will also be made for other hypotheses emerging from the public choice literature, (such as the fiscal illusion hypothesis) which are compatible with the demand-oriented approach developed in this study.

The analysis develops as follows. Some methodological issues are briefly addressed in section 2. The hypotheses to be tested for are formulated in section 3, where considerable space is given to represent dependent as well as independent variables on a cross-section basis, regardless of the actual feasibility of the analysis. Indeed, from this specific point of view, this chapter should more properly be considered a methodological exercise, the main aim of which is to stress the way in which the empirical investigation of the determinants of the pension demand should be developed, if data were available. The main aim is to highlight the nature of this issue and its several specific aspects from a methodological as well as an empirical

92

point of view. In section 4 the analysis will be extended to the time-series case and some further comments will be developed. The same *caveat* applies. Section 5 is devoted to commenting on the data, to developing a simple statistical analysis and to presenting the main OLS results reached so far. Brief concluding remarks are presented in section 6.

7.2 SOME PRELIMINARY METHODOLOGICAL QUESTIONS

7.2.1 The basic hypothesis stemming from the previous discussion is that the size of the pension system is positively related to the median age of the population because the older the median voter is, the higher will be the pension for which he will vote, this impact finding a likely limit in the economic constraints discussed in chapters 5 and 6. In testing for such an hypothesis other variables will be included in the equation to be estimated, under the assumption that the impact of these other factors is additive. In other words, it is assumed that the effect of ageing on the pension system does not change when the impact of other variables is taken into account. Indeed, the analysis of pressure groups developed in the last chapter would suggest that in order to provide a picture as close as possible to the real world, the median voter hypothesis needs to be further qualified. The variables used to express each relevant phenomenon, are listed in tables 7.1 and 7.2. The rationale underlying the choice of these variables will be exposed in the next paragraphs.

At the same time, it should be stressed that the list of variables (presented in tables 7.1 and 7.2) is not meant to be exhaustive, its object being only to point out how the different hypotheses could be specified, taking into account the indicators suggested in the literature to express similar hypotheses.

7.2.2 The choice of the type of test to be carried out is far from obvious. Detailed international data are scarce; moreover, considerable differences do exist across countries as far as the institutional features of different pension systems and the relative importance of the private and public sectors are concerned[4]. This argument would cast some doubts on the feasibility of carrying out a cross-section analysis. On the other hand, although the dynamic nature of the basic hypothesis might allow for the use of a time-series analysis, some problems are also related to this latter type of analysis. In fact, the evolution of social security systems is a complex long-term phenomenon which cannot easily be handled within the restricted scope of an empirical test, having as it does a limited time horizon (because of the lack of long-term homogeneous available data). Moreover, to test properly for such an evolution would call for the constructing of variables to represent concepts which it is difficult to quantify. The risk is that the incompleteness of the analysis might obscure the relevance and the explanatory power of the hypothesis under study.

Table 7.1. Dependent and independent variables – Cross-section analysis – OECD sample.

Variable name	Concept measured	Expected sign	Variable definition
1. PE/PPBEN GDP/L F	Pension Demand		Pension payments per potential beneficiary as percentage of GDP per capita (relevant population is total labour force).
2. PE/PPBEN WSPC	Pension Demand		Pension payments per potential beneficiary as percentage of wages and salaries per capita.
3. PMA	Ageing	+	Population median age.
*4. LE	Ageing	+	Life expectancy at the age of 65.
*5. DPP	Political participation by age	+	Ratio between the percentage of voting population over the retirement age and the percentage of voting population below such age.
6. HS	Individual preference for intergenerational redistribution	–	Average household size (degree of family solidarity).
*7. DRA	Individual preference for intergenerational redistribution	+	Total property/life insurance premiums as percentage of national income (degree of risk aversion).
8. CHGDP	Economic constraint	+	Percentage change of GDP (constant prices) in the period 1980–1985.
*9. DPSF	Existence of interest groups	–	Special schemes old age beneficiaires/benefits as percentage of general schemes old age beneficiaires/benefits (degree of pension systems fractionalisation).
*10. PIP	Existence of interest groups	–	Private insurance premiums as share of GDP (degree of private insurance influence).
11. SDR	Intensity of preferences (workers' reaction)	–	Population over 65 as percentage of employed (strong dependency ratio).
12. DTV	Fiscal perception	–	Percentage of social security contributions paid by employees (degree of tax visibility).

* Variables not used in the regression because of lack of available data.
1) OECD (1987), (1988a) and (1988d); 2) OECD (1987), (1988a) and (1988d); 3) United Nations (1985b); 4) *; 5) *; 6) Eurostat (1982), United Nations (1982) and (1985a); 7) *; 8) OECD (1987); 9) Eurostat (1977), this source was chosen because of the lack of more recent data; 10) *; 11) OECD (1988a) and United Nations (1985b); 12) OECD (1988b).

Therefore, given that no clear-cut argument stands for either type of test it seems better to try both. More precisely, a time-series regression is carried out with respect to Italy for the period (1960–1984). Moreover, cross-section regressions are also carried out with respect to 22 OECD countries. More particularly, given that observations on all the variables are not available for all countries, tests are carried out using different sub-samples[5].

7.3 THE PENSION EQUATION: CROSS-SECTION ANALYSIS

7.3.1 We seek to explain the differences in the evolution of pension systems in some OECD countries. All the variables (dependent as well as independent) used in this analysis are listed in table 7.1. No one measure can fully represent a complex phenomenon such as the evolution of pension systems. For this reason, it seems preferable to try several dependent variables, each one measuring a specific aspect of social security provision or change.

At first sight the most straightforward and aggregate measure of such a change would seem to be the level of social security spending; however, using such a variable would not throw any light on the issue under discussion, given that it increases as an (arithmetical) consequence of the fact that an ageing population implies more pensioners and, therefore, a higher level of total social security spending. The political decision-making process would not enter the story nor would the relevance of the median voter hypothesis be tested for.

The issue might be more conveniently addressed using a per capita measure, such as the average pension per capita (APPC). In this case, the ageing phenomenon, which is actually the independent variable, would no longer be included in the dependent variable. This variable will be further discussed in the next section where the time-series analysis is developed. In the cross-section analysis, in order to avoid the likely errors implied by reducing the absolute values to the same currency (for instance USA dollar) it seems preferable to look for other variables representing pension per capita as a percentage of other economic aggregates.

The dependent variable is obtainable using the results of recent OECD (1985) and (1988d) research on social expenditures[6]: pension payments per potential beneficiary is expressed as a percentage of GDP per capita, using labour force as population aggregate. This variable is designed to represent the claim for resources by aged people or, alternatively, the pension burden, on the labour force (PE/PPBEN / GDP/LF). Moreover, pension payments per potential beneficiary are also expressed as a percentage of wages and salaries per capita (PE/PPBEN / WSPC). This last variable seems the best approximation to the concept of the "pension burden" for the labour force. 1985 values at current as well as at constant prices are taken into account.

All the above mentioned variables have to be seen only as proxies of the actual aggregate of pension demand. In fact, some adjustments were requested especially in constructing the numerator. Broadly speaking, the numerator is underestimated given that potential beneficiaries are more numerous than actual beneficiaries; however, given that the coverage is extended to almost all the population, only minor errors are likely to arise. Moreover, potential beneficiaries are defined as people aged 65 and over although different retirement ages do exist in different countries. Since 65 is the most common retirement age in western countries, it was chosen for the whole sample. It implies that for those countries where workers retire earlier, the pension demand is underestimated.

It should be stressed that the above described variables focusing only upon pension provisions, do not fully capture the several dimensions of the wider demand for retirement provisions (additional services for old people, tax exemptions on pensions, supplementary payments). The above variables omit to take into account other items, which are complementary to and/or partially substitute for, and, therefore, do not represent the demand for retirement provisions in all its components. However, the non availability of suitable and comparable alternative data makes it impossible to construct a more complete variable and, therefore, we make the implicit, although not necessarily realistic[7] assumption that additional benefits (as well as allowances in pension taxation) do not vary across countries.

Nor are the specific features of the pension systems captured by the above mentioned dependent variables. Citizens, as a consequence of age trends, can be assumed to seek more satisfactory pension conditions through changes in the retirement age, women's retirement provisions, indexing systems, coverage extension, etc... In other words, our basic hypothesis might be more precisely delineated if we said that an increase in the median age of the population will imply an increase in the demand for pensions: at the first stage, this would imply an extension of pension coverage to those who were not receiving any pension in the previous period. But once the PAYG system has been established the demand for pensions is likely to be channelled into attempts to obtain legislative changes to increase the per capita pension level. Therefore, changes in the above mentioned features are likely to be requested by an ageing population. The system is likely to be always in a state of transition and, therefore, for the reasons already expounded, not many voters would be interested in discontinuing it.

7.3.2 Let us consider the independent variables, in order to make the hypothesis explicit. From the model set up in chapter 5[8] it follows that changes in pension provisions should be explained by changes in the median age of the population (PMA)[9].

Moreover, another aspect of the impact of ageing on the demand for pensions can be captured by taking into account life expectancy (LE). The longer the life expectancy at retirement age, the stronger will be the demand for pensions[10].

Finally, a further element connected with voting deserves some attention, i.e. the degree of political participation in relation to age (DPP). More precisely, an indicator of how political participation varies with age should be included in the equation. In fact, if the degree of political participation changes with age, (as seems likely) then, the "real" median age of the voting population differs from the "nominal" one. Therefore, any change in the degree of political participation through time will affect the demand for pensions. This variable might be constructed using the ratio between the percentage of population over the median age (or the retirement age) voting in general elections and the corresponding percentage for people below. So far, no available data have been found with which to construct this variable LE and DPP.

7.3.3 The preceding discussion argues that pension policy reflects the median aged voter's preferences. Still, within the individual preferences-oriented approach, other variables are worth mentioning. On the basis of the analysis developed in chapter 5, it should be pointed out that the choice between different social security rates is a choice between different levels of inter-generational redistribution,the extent of which can be limited by the existence of economic constraints.

Mutatis mutandis, the extensive past literature on the subject of public sector redistribution is useful for the purpose of deriving empirical hypotheses with respect to inter-generational redistribution.

An interesting explanation of income distribution as an outcome of individual choice is based on risk aversion. Friedman (1953) argues that risk aversion affects redistribution positively and leads to progressive tax structures[11]. *Mutatis mutandis,* the same argument might hold in the pension case. Indeed, risk aversion is likely to induce young workers to support social protection demand. When determining the empirical counterpart to such a theoretical variable, several indicators can be adopted. Differences in family structures might affect the amount of insurance a community is likely to purchase through social protection, given that social security can be considered a substitute for family obligations. More precisely, the household size (HS) is expected to be inversely related to the level of the demand for pensions[12]. The utilization of this variable, among the other things[13], however, may give rise to some problems, because multicollinearity is likely to occur[14]. Another variable to express the degree of risk aversion (DRA) is the ratio of premiums paid for property or life insurance to total national income. The higher such a ratio is, the higher the degree of risk aversion and the larger the demand for pensions. Available data to construct this latter variable have been found only with respect to the time-series test (see section 7.4)

Useful insights are also provided by the literature on the interdependence of utility functions and the distribution of income as a public good. More precisely, within this general framework, the demand for such a public good is expected to be, among other things, a positive function of the potential donor's income[15].

Adapting this general theoretical perspective to the narrower inter-generational context, this hypothesis seems to fit with the pension issue.

Moreover, such an hypothesis captures the role of economic factors in explaining the demand for pensions. The more resources are available in the community the less burdensome is the maintaining of the PAYG system and/or the improvement of retirees' conditions. The positive impact of economic growth on the demand for pensions can be captured by using the rate of change of GDP (at constant prices) in each country (CHGDP): the average (1980–1985) change of GDP will be used as a proxy for the level of economic growth in each country and a positive relationship is expected to hold between such a variable and the demand for pensions.

7.3.4 So far, voters have been assumed to act individually in the political market. No allowance was made for the role of preference intensity in political decision-making or for the role played by interest groups. In reality, political systems may weight weak preferences of large groups less heavily than intense preferences of small groups. Yet, as was argued in chapter 6, the characteristics of social security would suggest that there is room for interest groups to affect the political outcome. As was already pointed out, allowing for the existence of interest groups does not necessarily change the relationship between age and pension demand but qualifies it in a more realistic way.

The fact that the increase of benefits for a relatively small number of recipients occurs at the expense of a much larger working population makes it easy for the government to satisfy the recipients' demand. Beneficiaries' preferences, therefore, are likely to be given excessive weight. In public choice literature it is assumed that interest groups attempt to achieve favours for their membership by offering political support, i.e. votes to a party. As a result, in many cases, their action is assumed to favour the expansion of government activity. On these grounds it is predicted that the level of government outlays is greater the greater the number of interest groups in society. Mueller and Murrell (1986) provide empirical evidence to support this hypothesis.

Is it possible to transfer these general predictions to the pension case? As was already pointed out, the number of different pension schemes existing within social security systems can be used as a proxy for the number of interest groups supporting an increase in pensions. The argument goes as follows: the more schemes are in existence the greater the political demand exerted by groups representing narrow categories, (to obtain favourable pension provisions, privileges and so on) is likely to be.

In analogy with the literature on pressure groups we might say that pension provisions are likely to increase the greater the number of existing pension schemes. Since it is very difficult to calculate the number of interest groups existing in social security systems, such an hypothesis can be expressed by measuring the degree of pension system fractionalisation (DPSF) as the percentage of old age benefits paid by special schemes[16]. No available data have been found with respect to the cross-section test.

A somewhat different aspect of the pressure groups issue can be explored by looking at the existence and the relevance of those groups, which contrast to the increase of pension provisions within a PAYG system, namely private insurance and financial companies providing pensions as a complement or in addition to compulsory public pension schemes. The less advantageous is the economic treatment meted out within the PAYG system, the more attractive private pension funds become. The effectiveness of private pension schemes in "controlling" the pension system is likely to depend on their dimension and on their market power. The problem, however, is to find suitable indicators to express this phenomenon. The share of total private insurance premiums of GDP (PIP) might serve as a proxy to represent the overall influence of insurance companies: the higher the value of PIP the lower is the expected demand for pensions. So far, no available data have been found to test for this hypothesis.

The above mentioned variables expressing the pressure groups hypothesis would capture only the intra-generational redistribution phenomenon, regardless of the age of the population. Their implication is that, assuming that the median age is unchanged, the greater the number and the relevance of pressure groups is, the higher public expenditure for pensions is likely to be. No reference is made to the inter-generational redistribution issue as expressed by the competition between retirees' groups and workers. However, major difficulties arise when this latter phenomenon has to be expressed[17]. Firstly, not all the groups operating in this field are formally identifiable and, what is more, no unambiguous measure of their strength can be found. Further and more satisfactory developments have yet to be investigated.

However, even if such a phenomenon cannot be expressed looking at the number or the strength of pressure groups, some qualifications in this sense can still be introduced, recalling the theoretical considerations developed in chapter 6. More precisely, it was stressed that increasing deadweight costs would encourage the resistance of workers to social security and, other things being equal, would discourage further increases of pension provisions. Such an hypothesis can be tested for using, as a proxy for deadweight costs, the ratio between pensioners and workers, which we might call the "strong dependency ratio" (SDR). The higher such a ratio is, the higher the individual burden deriving from social security will be[18]. As a consequence, on the strength of the above considerations, a negative relationship is expected to hold between (SDR) and pension demand. Such a negative relationship can be justified on strictly economic grounds: the higher SDR is, the smaller the amount of resources available for redistribution. In other words, other things being equal, i.e. the median age, high values of SDR may impose economic constraints on the demand for pensions. Although the use of this indicator offers useful insights for an investigation of the role of pressure groups, the likely multicollinearity problems arising from using it should not be over-looked.

7.3.5 Finally, another issue to be dealt with is the occurrence of fiscal misperception. As is well known, social security contributions[19] are split into two parts, paid by both the employers and the employees and it is widely recognised that such a differentiation is a fiction, the burden being entirely born by the workers. The contributions paid by employers, however, are less "visible" for the taxpayers, i.e. for the workers, and, therefore, any change in the relative size of these two parts would affect the "price" of social security, as perceived by workers. The analysis of fiscal perception developed in chapter 3 would suggest that any decrease in the "visible" price (or, alternatively, any increase in the "invisible" price with respect to the overall price) would raise the demand for pensions, regardless of the age of the taxpayer. This phenomenon might be conveniently expressed by an indicator of tax visibility (DTV), such as the percentage of total contributions[20] paid by employees[21]: the lower such a ratio is, the lower the perceived social security price[22] and the larger the pension demand.

7.4 THE PENSION EQUATION: TIME-SERIES ANALYSIS

7.4.1 This section is aimed at extending the preceding analysis to the time-series case. Dependent as well as independent variables used in the time-series regression are listed in table 7.2. No major changes occur with respect to the cross-section case; however, a few comments are still in order.

Let us begin with an analysis of the dependent variables. ISTAT (1983) and (1988) provide data for the average pension per capita (APPC) on a long-term basis (1960–1984) both in current prices and constant prices values[23]. The latter seems to be more interesting than the former; because of the length of the period under study, monetary values are likely to misrepresent the "real generosity" of the system. Apart from the absolute value of pension per capita, variables representing pension benefits as a share of individual wealth are also used.

More precisely, in analogy with the cross-section analysis, two more variables are constructed: AAPC is considered as a share of GDP per capita, using as population aggregate the labour force (APPC / GDP/LF). Moreover, to focus more closely upon the inter-generational redistributive issue, the ratio between pension per capita and wages per capita (APPC/WSPC) is also taken into account.

These variables, when compared with the analogous ones constructed for the cross-section case would seem to provide a better representation of the pension demand concept. In fact, smaller adjustments are required as far as the retirement age and the amount of pension per capita are concerned.

100

Table 7.2. Dependent and independent variables – Time-series analysis (Italy, 1960–1984).

Variable name	Concept measured	Expected sign	Variable definition
1. APPC	Pension Demand		Average pension per capita.
2. APPC GDP/LF	Pension Demand		APPC as share of GDP per capita (relevant population is labour force).
3. APPC/WSPC	Pension Demand		APPC as share of wages and salaries per capita.
4. PMA	Ageing	+	Population median age.
*5. LE	Ageing	+	Life expectancy at the age of 65.
*6. DPP	Political participation by age	+	Ratio between the percentage of voting population over the retirement age and the percentage of voting population below such age.
7. HS	Individual preference for intergenerational redistribution	–	Average household size (degree of family solidarity).
8. DRA	Individual preference for intergenerational redistribution	+	Property/life insurance premiums as share of national income (degree of risk aversion).
9. CHGDP	Economic constraints	+	Percentage change of GDP.
10. TIME	Time	+	The number of observation periods from a starting year onwards.
11. DPSF	Existence of interest groups	–	Special schemes old age beneficiaires/benefits as percentage of general schemes old age beneficiaires/benefits (degree of pension systems fractionalisation).
*12. DLP	Existence of interest groups	+	Number of laws and acts on pensions (degree of legislative production).
*13. PIP	Existence of interest groups	–	Private insurance premiums as share of GDP (degree of private insurance power).
14. SDR	Existence of youngsters' interest groups	–	POP 65+ as percentage of employed (strong dependency ratio).
*15. DTV	Fiscal perception	–	Percentage of social security contributions paid by employees (degree of tax visibility).

* Variables not yet tested for because of lack of available data.
1) ISTAT (1983) and (1988); 2) ISTAT (1983), (1986), (1987) and (1988); 3) ISTAT (1983), (1987) and (1988); 4) AA.VV. (1983) and ISTAT (1985); 5) *; 6)*; 7) ISTAT (A) and (B); 8) ISTAT (A); 9) ISTAT (1987); 10) Time; 11) *; 12) *; 13) *; 14) AA.VV. (1983), ISTAT (1985) and (1986); 15) *.

7.4.2 The ageing phenomenon is represented by the population median age (PMA).

As in the cross-section analysis, no data are available to represent the degree of political participation by age (DPP).

A better representation of the individual preferences-oriented approach to redistribution is possible for the time-series case. More precisely, the degree of risk aversion (DRA) is represented by the share of national income paid for property or life insurance premiums. The other variable previously proposed to test for the individual oriented approach,i.e. household size (HS), is also included. The percentage change of GDP (CHGDP) is calculated at current as well as at constant prices. This variable, representing the willingness to pay for inter-generational redistribution, allows for taking into account the impact of economic constraints on the fulfilment of unfunded obligations.

The role played through time by economic conditions can be expressed using another variable such as time (T) as a proxy for economic growth. A positive relationship is expected to hold among T and CHGDP variables and the demand for pensions.

7.4.3 More comments are needed to apply the interest group approach to the Italian time-series analysis. In fact, the most peculiar feature of the Italian pension system is the presence of several pension schemes, characterised by relevant differences as far as the age of retirement, social security contributions and replacement rates are concerned. Indeed, potentially, the pressure group hypothesis would seem to play a significant role in explaining the development of pension demand in Italy.

Of course, in testing for this hypothesis the same difficulties outlined for the cross-section analysis arise, as far as the availability of data is concerned. However, since only one country is under study, alternative, although less straightforward, data might be found more easily. On the other hand, the dimension of the pressure group phenomenon in the pension system is such[24] that alternative indicators seem worth trying. Owing to the major legislative changes which occurred in the mid-seventies[25], no homogeneous data for different pension schemes expenditure as well as for the number of retirees covered by each scheme are available for the period 1960–1984. Therefore, the degree of the pension system fractionalisation (DPSF) cannot be measured over all the period for the overall expenditure. Such an indicator has been constructed taking into account only INPS (National Institute for Social Security), the most important social security institution of the system[26], the public sector pension funds and an aggregate measure of the other minor funds. An inverse relationship is expected to hold between DPSF and the demand for pension; in fact, the higher the value of the indicator the lower the degree of fractionalisation and, therefore, according to the pressure group hypothesis recalled above, the demand for pensions is lower, other things being equal.

Looking at the entire system, alternative proxies can be used (in addition to PIP variable) to represent the pressure group phenomenon. Within the interest group approach, the legislative decision-making process is assumed to be devoted to satisfying pressure groups' demand. Starting from this perspective, we might easily assume that the larger the number of pressure groups or the more active they are the "busier" the legislator is likely to be and, therefore, the larger the number of laws and, more generally, legislative acts produced by politicians in response to pressure groups' demand for pension benefits, privileges and so on. Therefore, an indicator of legislative production in the pension issue (DLP) might be used as a proxy for the presence and the activity of pressure groups. Such an indicator might be constructed using the number of laws and acts produced each year to regulate the pension issue. Given that a positive relationship is expected to hold between DLP and the number of pressure groups, a positive relationship should also link DLP and the demand for pension. So far, no available data have been found to construct DLP.

So far, the intra-generational redistributive aspect of the pension issue has been examined. Looking at the inter-generational dimension, no further comments are to be added to those developed in the preceding section. In fact, the lack of available data does not allow for including in the time-series analysis other variables than SDR.The same *caveat* already outlined applies.

Finally, in testing for the fiscal illusion hypothesis no further variables are proposed; the same indicators proposed for the cross-section analysis should be used in the time-series case[27]. So far available data do not allow for constructing the suggested indicator over the period (1960–1984).

7.5 OLS RESULTS

7.5.1 In the previous section some testable hypotheses were discussed and several variables were listed.

Starting with the cross-section analysis some comments are in order. Given the small number of observations there are problems of testing; therefore, the conclusions must be drawn with caution from the OLS results. On the other hand, such a limit seems to be unavoidable, given the lack of degrees of freedom. The choice is between testing, acknowledging the possibility of errors or not testing at all. Bearing these problems in mind, let us look at the OLS results.

The estimated equations for the OECD sample are listed in table 7.3[28]. The log-linear form has been chosen because it showed a better performance. Given the tentative nature of the results provided by the OLS regression, it seems better to list only the most representative, or rather the least unsatisfactory, estimated equations. It is true that this procedure is somewhat arbitrary and that the overall spectrum of results would provide a better, and more objective, representation of our achievements. Again, the nature of the result may justify such a choice.

Table 7.3. Cross-section Analysis – OECD Sample (1985). Regression Results (t-statistics in parentheses).

		$\bar{R}^2$ F	c	PMA	CHGDP	DTV
a)	*22 observations*					
1	PE/PBEN GDP/LF	0.18 5.66	−0.44 (0.27)	1.10* (2.38)		
2	PE/PBEN GDP/LF	0.14 2.75	−0.70 (0.38)	1.16* (2.26)	0.04 (0.32)	
b)	*17 observations*					
3	PE/PBEN GDP/LF	0.22 5.65	−1.16 (0.60)	1.30* (2.38)		
4	PE/PBEN GDP/LF	0.18 2.79	−1.62 (0.73)	1.42* (2.31)	−0.06 (0.47)	
5	PE/PBEN GDP/LF	0.19 2.29	−1.10 (0.49)	1.50* (2.43)	−0.05 (0.36)	−0.22 (1.10)

The estimated equations refer to different samples[29], given that data for all the variables are not available for the full sample. Among the variables representing the same phenomenon, only the most representative have been chosen. The first general observation is that the estimated equations perform poorly, as is shown by the low values of the adjusted correlation coefficient and of the F-statistics, though these are partially justified by the cross-section nature of the regression.

Equations 1, and 3 show the influence of the demographic factor: the hypothesis regarding the impact of the median age on pensions can be accepted. The PMA variable turns out to be significant and with the correct sign. Having tested for stability, we arrive at the conclusion that the coefficients are stable and that they imply the existence of a stable relationship between dependent and independent variables.

The fit of the equation is not improved when the impact of economic factors is tested for. CHGDP, though not significant, often shows the correct sign.

In the case of the interest group hypothesis, the lack of available data on the actual relevance of interest groups in OECD countries[30], does not allow for testing for such hypothesis correctly[31].

Finally, the fiscal hypothesis does not allow for more satisfactory conclusions. DTV, although of the correct sign, does not turn out to be significant. One possible explanation for this poor performance might be that it does not directly measure the visibility of the pension burden but a wider concept such as the social security burden visibility.

To conclude, the overall explanatory power of the equations is poor as is their significance. Further developments are needed in two main areas: other variables should be included in the equation given that the low values of the adjusted correlation coefficient would suggest that some relevant explanatory variables have been omitted; more satisfactory indicators should be constructed to express the fiscal perception and the interest groups issues.

7.5.2 Turning to a consideration of the time-series analysis, some comments are in order. The first problem to deal with is the role of time. Among the various methods suggested in the literature to take into account the influence of time on the dependent variable, the introduction of time as a variable has been chosen. It is better to stress two relevant factors:
- such a choice implies that there is an autonomous trend experienced by the dependent variable, the coefficients of the explanatory variables remaining constant;
- time, being a proxy for economic growth, expresses also the influence of economic factors on the demand for pensions.

Table 7.4 shows relevant differences in the performances of estimated equations according to which dependent variable is used and, therefore, which phenomenon is tested for. Equations a) of each group represent the demand for pension as expressed by the average pension per capita while equations b) represent the pension burden as expressed by the average pension per capita as a ratio of wages per capita.

As a first general statement, from the performance of equations 5a) and 5b) in table 7.4, it follows that the average pension per capita seems more sensitive to time trends than the pension burden. The reason may be found in the fact that through time, and as the country becomes richer, each component of the community enjoys an increase in welfare: as a consequence, the growth of the dependent variable is likely to be determined by exogenous forces rather than by explanatory variables. And in fact, the performance of the variables representing the demographic, the pressure groups and the voluntary redistribution hypotheses is worsened when time is explicitly introduced into equations sub a): all of them turn out to be of the wrong sign and not significant[32]. The reason is that the increase of average pension per capita can be considered mainly the result of the increased "size of the pie" which was the result of the economic growth of the (1960–1984) period. Nothing is said about the inter-generational redistribution. In this case, therefore, the main determinant of the increase of pension per capita seems to be time as a proxy for economic and social development rather than demographic and political factors.

Different issues arise when the determinants of the pension demand, expressed in terms of the pension burden (or replacement rate) are examined. Such a variable represents the demand for pension in a more specific way: in fact, it mainly represents the demand for inter-generational redistribution, between retirees and

Table 7.4. Times-series Analysis – Italy (1960–1984). Regression Results (t-statistics in parentheses).

		$\bar{R}^2$ F DW	c	PMA	CHGDP	DRA	DPSF	TIME
1a)	APPC	0.98 565.98 2.09	−25.86 (2.77)	9.32* (3.50)				
1b)	APPC WSPC	0.78 40.67 2.01	−6.79 (1.61)	2.98* (2.47)				
2a)	APPC	0.98 390.29 1.99	−25.90 (2.58)	9.32* (3.26)	0.47 (1.25)			
2b)	APPC WSPC	0.79 28.03 1.90	−7.29 (1.68)	3.12* (2.51)	0.43 (1.11)			
3a)	APPC	0.98 327.0 2.46	−24.11 (3.53)	8.73* (4.45)	0.41 (1.13)	−0.28 (1.79)		
3b)	APPC WSPC	0.83 22.69 1.92	−3.86 (1.11)	2.06 (2.02)	0.41 (0.93)	−0.24 (1.78)		
4a)	APPC	0.98 262.72 2.58	−24.32 (4.09)	8.63* (4.96)	0.59 (1.44)	−0.23 (1.49)	−0.54 (1.12)	
4b)	APPC WSPC	0.79 17.26 1.91	−4.21 (1.08)	2.20 (1.83)	0.37 (0.78)	−0.26 (1.86)	0.15 (0.30)	
5a)	APPC	0.98 242.41 2.42	19.09 (0.98)	−3.87 (0.69)	0.27 (0.61)	−0.15 (1.28)	0.36 (0.62)	0.07* (2.48)
5b)	APPC WSPC	0.82 17.37 2.19	−40.48 (1.96)	12.63* (2.13)	0.69 (1.54)	−0.25 (1.93)	−0.62 (0.91)	−0.05 (1.67)

workers. It is on this variable that age exerts its effects *via* the political process. The pressure groups and the risk aversion variables are assumed to act through the same process. The inter-generational redistribution, as determined by the replacement rate, does not seem to represent a strong time-trend phenomenon suggesting that the hypotheses discussed above are likely to play a role in explaining the evolution of the pension system in Italy.

As table 7.4 shows, the estimated equations, though still to be improved, are apparently satisfactory, both statistically and theoretically. The adjusted correlation coefficients are fairly high, suggesting a good predictive power. The values of F show that the relationship denoted by the regression is significant. Also in this case the equations are in logarithmic form because such a form showed the best performance. Equations are already corrected for autocorrelation[33] and the Durbin-Watson values are such that the null hypothesis of no autocorrelation can be accepted. At the same time, the test for stability showed that the coefficients remained stable over time. Multicollinearity problems seem to remain: though some variables have not been used to reduce the occurrence of multicollinearity, still some wild values of the estimated coefficients would suggest that these problems have not been completely overcome.

The median age variable (PMA) turns out to be statistically significant and of the correct sign, in almost all the equations, giving some support to the median voter hypothesis.

The performance of the other variables is less satisfactory. The "voluntary redistribution" hypothesis cannot be accepted. In fact, the DRA variable turns out to be of the wrong sign and never significant[34]. As a result, the impact of the individual voluntary attitude toward redistribution does not receive any clear confirmation.

Nor are decisive results obtained when CHGDP is tested for: though of the correct sign, it does not turn out statistically significant. Nevertheless, the result suggests that this line of enquiry is worth exploring and that economic factors might be relevant to an explanation of the evolution of pension systems.On the other hand, the results obtained through the empirical analysis do not allow us to support the idea expounded in chapter 5, that economic factors constrain the evolution of pension systems and that, as a consequence, ageing, enforcing these constraints, might even exert a negative influence on pension demand[35]. Indeed, this idea is weakened in the Italian system where the external financial intervention constitutes a relevant share of the PAYG budget. In this case, as in most other european countries, old age pension provisions are subsidised with government general revenue and, therefore, ageing does not necessarily impose an extra-burden on workers only but on taxpayers as a whole. As a consequence, the explanatory power of economic constraints in our equation is less, compared to the theoretical one.

Finally, the role of pressure groups has been explored. The impact of pressure groups upon intra-generational redistribution has been tested for using as explanatory variable the degree of fractionalisation (DPSF). The hypothesis that the fractionalisation of the system positively affects the demand for pension does not receive strong support from the regression; in fact, DPSF turns out to be of the correct sign but not significant. This result, however, might depend upon the indicator and does not enable us to reject the pressure group hypothesis as such. Indeed, on the basis of the available data, the indicator has been constructed according too much weight to the major pension scheme, i.e. INPS, (and to the various special schemes within it). The fractionalisation of the rest of the system has not been adequately taken into account, given that for the minor schemes only an aggregate measure was available. For this reason, the indicator is likely to underestimate the actual degree of fractionalisation of the system and its poor performance does not allow us to reject the pressure group hypothesis as such[36].

To finish, a concluding remark is in order. Not all the explanatory variables listed in table 7.2 have been tested for, either because of the difficulties encountered in constructing some indicators or owing to the lack of available data. For instance, the fiscal illusion hypothesis has not been tested for because of the lack of homogeneous data for the overall period. The above results, therefore, might be considered more encouraging than the figures show. In fact, improvements might be obtained by including more explanatory variables in the equation. Further developments are required in this direction, which seems to be a fruitful line of enquiry.

The first tentative result stemming from the analysis so far is that ageing can be considered a relevant factor for explaining the growth of the demand for pension in Italy, during the period 1960–1984. Economic factors do not seem to have exerted a significant influence; the fact that a large share of the Italian pension system is subsidised with government general revenue is likely to weaken the impact of economic constraints. This does not exclude the possibility that the other explanatory variables might also have played a relevant role. Further investigation is needed.

7.6 CONCLUDING REMARKS

7.6.1 Rather than seeking to draw conclusion, this section aims at highlighting the insights deriving from the results presented above and at outlining the areas for further development. In fact, so far, empirical results do not allow for the drawing of clear-cut conclusions.

Firstly, it seems important to point out that differences occur when the same hypotheses are tested for one country or across countries. These differences may depend on many factors: the eventual inadequacy of the regression model employed and the very nature of the issue under study are two possible explanations. Leaving aside the former, which requires the analysis of statistical problems which are outside the scope of this paper, let us concentrate further on the latter.

The doubts casted at the beginning of this chapter upon the validity of a cross-section exercise would seem to be confirmed. Thus, a crucial feature of the pension issue is stressed: i.e. the complex relationships existing between such an issue and the political, economic and social framework characterising each country. The 1985 pension system is the result of a long and complex process, the length of which varies across countries, according to their economic and political evolution. Therefore, it is difficult to ascertain how many of the differences in the demand for pension can be accounted for by explanatory variables rather than by each country's socio-economic and political features. On the other hand, these considerations would provide further support for the opportunity of dealing with the pension issue using a public choice approach, which seems the most suitable for grasping the complexity of the evolution of social security systems.

After the general considerations outlined above, other comments are in order. Although the results do not allow us to draw clear-cut conclusions, some arguments can still be advanced. The demographic median voter hypothesis receives support in both cases, in the cross-section as well as in the time-series analysis. The other hypotheses, those of "voluntary redistribution", pressure groups and fiscal illusion, cannot be rejected or accepted on the basis of the regression carried out so far: development of other indicators is required to provide further evidence.

NOTES

1. In the model presented above the extent of such an effect is likely to be limited by the substitution effect arising as a consequence of a change in the "return" on pensions.
2. In fact, they do not take into account the existence of counterbalancing substitution effects.
3. Maser (1985) has studied the impact that the demographic characteristics of the population exert on constitutional decisions.
4. The difficulties have been recently stressed by Heller, Hemming and Kohnert (1986).
5. Within the OECD sample some interesting insights can be derived by looking at the EEC countries. The reason for taking the EEC specifically into account is that Eurostat provides useful statistical information which enables us to construct independent variables representing the interest groups phenomenon (see note 30). Analogous information is not available for OECD countries.
6. In this OECD research, the changes in social security expenditures are decomposed into three main items: the demographic ratio, the eligibility ratio and the transfer ratio. The first item corresponds to the "relevant" population (i.e. people aged over 65) as a ratio of the total population; the second represents the beneficiaries per "relevant" population (PBEN/POP65+) and the third is a measure of the "generosity", corresponding to per capita pension payments as a percentage of GDP per head (PE/PBEN / GDP/POP). This approach can be expressed by the following identity:

$$\frac{PE}{GDP} = \frac{POP65+}{POP} \cdot \frac{PBEN}{POP65+} \cdot \frac{PE/PBEN}{GDP/POP}$$

where:
   PE = total public expenditure on pensions;
   POP65+ = population aged 65 and over;

POP = total population;
PBEN = pension beneficiaries.

For the sake of comparability a homogeneous age group has been selected (people aged 65 and above) although in many countries retirement age is lower.

7. As has been pointed out in an earlier OECD study (1976) differences do exist across countries. Pensions are usually taxable but tax rates vary across countries and there are exemptions for certain "basic" public schemes as well as abatements for those over the age of 65. Analogously, differences do exist as far as occupational schemes and private pensions are concerned. Unfortunately, information on these aspects is scanty and does not allow us to take them explicitly into account. However, as the OECD report outlines, the above mentioned differences do not seem to be large enough to invalidate the analysis.

8. The relationship between the rate of population increase and the median age was dealt with in chapter 5, Appendix.

9. Alternatively, the median age of the voting population (VPMA) might be used. This variable can be constructed only arbitrarily, because of the differences existing among countries with respect to the voting age. Another less straightforward variable representing the ageing phenomenon is the rate of population annual change (RPAC); a negative relationship is expected to exist between such variable and the demand for pensions.

10. In fact, within the life-cycle perspective adopted in chapter 5, longer expected length of life after retirement implies, *ceteris paribus,* an increase in the present value of future pension payments and, therefore, a greater tendency to vote, in the present, for increased contribution rate.

11. The reasoning is that the tax structure plays a role similar to private insurance when private market fails. If the degree of risk aversion increases with income, the income of the community might have a positive effect on tax progressivity.

12. It is interesting to note that such a relationship does not necessarily hold when other aspects of social security programmes are taken into account. Beneficiaries of social security programmes are not only retired workers but also spouses and children. The occurrence of relevant changes in the structure of families, because of the growing phenomenon of being single, might imply an inverse relationship between family size and social security demand: in fact, being single reduces the (perceived) worth of social security in terms of money (Yung-Ping Chen, 1982). On the other hand, Breyer, Graf and Schulenburg (1987), taking family as financial and decision-making unit, suggest that those who bear the burden of raising more than the average number of children are most reluctant to pay for the retirement benefits of the childless singles.

13. Actually some difficulties would be encountered in calculating such a variable: data provided by Eurostat (1982), and the United Nations (1982 and 1985a) do not refer to the same year but for some countries there is a gap of up to five years.

14. Multicollinearity is likely to occur between median age and household size, because both variables are affected by the same demographic factor, i.e. the rate of population growth. For instance, *ceteris paribus,* the higher the birth rate, the lower the median age and, at the same time, the larger the household size is likely to be.

15. For a discussion of this issue, see Greene (1986). Actually, two other hypotheses are put forward in the same literature (the so-called Paretian approach to redistribution): redistribution is positively affected by i) the pre-existing level of income dispersion and ii) the size of the community, if the free-rider problem varies with the community size. These two hypotheses do not seem to be relevant in the case of pension. For instance, inequality as such does not fit with the unfunded obligations issue or, at least, with our basic hypothesis that age is the major determinant of demand for pensions. Indeed, present inequalities in income distribution are unlikely to alter the demand for pensions given that other means of redistribution, in the present, are more likely to be sought. Nor does the community size seem to be significant given that in the pension case the

"relevant" community and its size are already well defined, i.e. the labour force. Any change in this size, for instance, occurring because of unemployment changes, does not affect the free-rider phenomenon. Such a change may, however, have an impact on the strength of the economic constraints.

16. According to the Eurostat (1977) definition, special schemes are "basic schemes which protect specific occupational groups or persons working in certain branches of the economy (mining, shipping, farming, etc...) which differ from the general schemes in that specific rules apply to the granting and financing of benefits. Accordingly, the benefits provided under a special scheme take the place of those provided under the general scheme". To measure such a phenomenon,as an alternative to DPSF, a dummy variable (DV) can be used, equal to 1, when special schemes do exist. Homogeneous data to construct variables based on special social security schemes for the cross-section analysis are available only for EEC countries and, therefore, OLS results are presented in note 30 only for this sub-sample.

17. The literature on interest groups is not very helpful; it does not provide indicators suitable for adoption. Murrel (1984) has carried on an empirical analysis on the factors affecting the formation of interest groups. Socio-economic development is one of the factors which have been found to have a significant impact on group formation. The proxies used by Murrel to test for such an hypothesis are not suitable for testing for pension demand because they do not allow for any inter-generational distinction. A proxy for the level of development, namely for elders' information level, can be given by the years of education experienced by this segment of population (EYE). A positive relationship is expected to hold between such a variable, implying a larger number of old age interest groups, and the pension demand. No available homogeneous data have been found to test for this variable. The other variable which had been found significant in explaining group formation, i.e. population, does not fit with the case under study because of the multicollinearity problems which might arise with respect to the median age.

18. It is assumed that social security systems are purely PAYG systems, i.e. that the pension budget is balanced. If this is not the case, the argument does not necessarily hold, given that any increase in pension provisions, as a consequence of an increase in the number of pensioners, might be financed out of the general revenue and, therefore,no extra-burden would be imposed on workers. Indeed, as Stein (1980) points out, most European industrial countries subsidise old age insurance programmes with government revenues.

19. Data do not allow for making a distinction between social security contributions made for pension purposes and for other income maintenance purposes or for health.

20. It should be noted that we are talking about the statutory social security rates. In the literature it is claimed that the statutory rates may overstate the effective rates once the links between social security contributions and benefits are allowed for. The extent of such an overstatement is controversial; it is considered quite relevant by Burkhauser and Turner (1985) whereas its dimensions are considered less relevant by Browning (1985). One can, however, question whether workers know enough about the social security system and about their own position to be influenced by the effective rather than the statutory rates. Moreover, effective rates are influenced by the discount rates chosen by individuals and, therefore, a wide range of estimated effective rates does exist. For the above reasons, and given that it is not feasible to estimate the effective rates across countries, the statutory rates are used.

21. It might be pointed out that relevant differences do exist across countries in methods of financing their social benefits. In some countries, not only social security contributions but also other taxes are levied for the same purpose. In order to take into account these differences the above mentioned DTV variable should be "adjusted", by including in the denominator not only social security contributions but all the sources of social security revenues (apart from government general revenue). However, this "adjusted" indicator implies a different problem: while it is commonly accepted that the

employer's contributions are less visible than the employees' ones this is not necessarily the case with respect to other sources of revenue included in the "adjusted" denominator; therefore, lower values of ADTV (adjusted degree of tax visibility) variable need not imply underperception of the fiscal burden if, for instance, the other sources of revenue included in the "adjusted" denominator are indirect taxes. Available data do not allow for identifying these revenues: the OECD (1988b) provides "Country tables on the financing of social security benefits" where the sources of financing other than contributions are: i) other taxes, ii) voluntary contributions to government and iii) compulsory contributions to the private sector.

22. Actually, other indicators of fiscal illusion can be found in the level of social security price (SSP) or of social security deficit (SSD). Both represent the same phenomenon. The former shows the percentage of social security expenditure financed out of contributions; the latter represents the percentage of social security expenditure financed out of general government financial intervention. It should be pointed out that these indicators, as well as all the others just described, representing the fiscal misperception phenomenon, refer to the entire social security system and not to the pension system alone; therefore, they merely give an approximation of the "perceived price" of pensions. Since old age benefits are the major component of social security expenditure, they can be considered acceptable "proxies" to represent the perception of the "pension price". Recalling the conventional public choice fiscal illusion literature, it is reasonable to argue that the less close is the relationship between the service and its price, because of the occurrence of deficit financing, the less is the tax burden perceived by taxpayers and, therefore, the higher the public expenditure demand. Thus, a positive relationship is expected to hold between SSD and the demand for pension, while a negative relationship is expected between such a demand and SSP.

23. These data do not refer to the overall pension system but only to *Public Administration Institutions,* including the most important social security funds as well as civil servant pension funds. The aggregate *Private Institutions* is not included. However, given that in 1984 *Public Administration Institutions* expenditure accounted for about 90% of the overall expenditure for pension, the aggregate seems to represent the system satisfactorily.

24. The institutional features of the Italian pension system are described by Panella (1982).

25. The major legislative changes introduced since the second World War are described by ISTAT (1981, pp.1-7). The main streams can be identified:
   – the extension of social security to increasing sectors of the population;
   – the improvement and the enlargement of pension treatments.

26. Such an institution includes several special and heterogeneous schemes going from private sector employees to self-employed, agricultural workers, etc. According to ISTAT (1986), in 1983 pensions paid by INPS accounted for 74.5 per cent of the total amount of pensions. Actually, this figure includes not only old age pensions but also survivors' and disability pensions paid by INPS; therefore, it is likely to overestimate the relative weight of INPS as far as the specific sector of old age pensions is concerned. Two different measures of DPSF are tested for $DPSF = \sum Xi^2$ where Xi is the percentage of total pension expenditure provided by the pension scheme i and $DPSF/B = \sum Bi^2$ where Bi is the percentage of the total pension beneficiaries belonging to scheme i. Actually, this index is a modified version of a Herfindahl index of concentration applied to social security funds' structure: the higher the value of DPSF and of DPSF/B the higher the concentration of the system and, therefore, the less widespread the interest group's phenomenon is supposed to be.

27. In this case,since the analysis is confined to one country, where the social security system is financed mainly out of contributions and government financial intervention, there is no need for adjustments (see note 21).

28. The equations listed in table 7.3 have been estimated both at current and constant prices. No major differences arise: therefore, only the current prices equations are reported, given that they perform slightly better.

29. Sample sub b) is obtained from sample sub a) excluding Finland, Norway, Sweden, Australia and New Zealand.

30. The interest group hypothesis has also been tested, using the already mentioned variables DV and DPSF with a sub-sample formed by EEC countries; both variables exhibit the correct sign but do not turn out to be significant. Of course, the small size does not allow us to obtain firm predictions; it only broadly indicates that the interest group hypothesis should not be rejected as such and that it might provide useful lines of inquiry, once it is correctly specified. For the EEC sample the following equations have been estimated;

$$\frac{PE/PBEN}{GDP/LF} = -\underset{(0.40)}{13.98} + \underset{(1.28)}{1.35}\ PMA - \underset{(0.091)}{0.023}\ DPSF$$

$$\bar{R}^2 = 0.23$$
$$F = 0.91$$

$$\frac{PE/PBEN}{GDP/LF} = -\underset{(0.29)}{10.54} + \underset{(1.11)}{1.22}\ PMA + \underset{(0.35)}{2.18}\ DV$$

$$\bar{R}^2 = 0.25$$
$$F = 0.98.$$

31. SDR,the only indicator tested for, shows a poor performance, deriving also from the fact that a relationship does exist with the median age, giving rise to multicollinearity problems. In fact; SDR turns out to be of the wrong sign in contrast with the idea, previously supported, that increasing deadweight costs (deriving from high values of SDR) would encourage the reactions of younger generations. The positive sign exhibited by SDR would suggest that the demographic effect prevails.

32. Analogous results were obtained when first differences were used to take into account the role of time.

33. Autocorrelation is not unusual in time-series data where time trends can be expected to play an important role. To correct for autocorrelation, equations have been estimated after transforming the original data using the Cochrane-Orcutt method.

34. HS has not been used because of the above mentioned multicollinearity problems.

35. See equation [13] in chapter 5.

36. On the other hand, SDR turned out not to be significant and of the wrong sign. In evaluating these results the likely relationship between this variable and the median age should not be overlooked.

8. Conclusions

8.1 Ideally, a concluding chapter is meant to offer a comprehensive list of clear and satisfying solutions to the problems raised throughout the preceding chapters. Unfortunately, the problems of social policy rarely allow for such a result. Moreover, the nature of this study itself does not make it possible to offer straightforward solutions. In fact, as it has been already pointed out, it is meant as a collection of essays on various aspects of the interlocking areas of social security and public choice, rather than as an unitary analysis of one specific issue within this area. As a consequence, this study is more suitable for raising issues than it is for offering clear-cut answers. Therefore, the object of this final short chapter is more modest than it would be in an ideal world. Nevertheless, in the following pages an attempt will be made to highlight some of the arguments considered earlier, to illustrate their relevance to specific aspects of pension policy and, where possible, to suggest ways in which the issue of reforms might be addressed.

8.2 The first argument to emerge is that PAYG systems, though not committed to ensure any actuarial equivalence between contributions and benefits, do give rise to obligations on the part of those who have contributed to the system. These obligations may be considered as implicit debt, based on a "social contract" between generations, the main features of which are uncertainty and flexibility. Given the social nature of this contract, government serves as intermediary and political guarantor for securing the performance of the underlying obligation. The recognition that unfunded obligations imply the existence of implicit debt does provide a conceptual support to include pension obligations in the public choice debate on public debt and to examine its policy implications. Interesting lines of enquiry stem from the implicit debt argument and some of them have been investigated in this study.

The analysis of the factors affecting individuals' perception of funded and unfunded debt liability highlights the fact that in both cases misperception is likely to occur. Relevant differences do arise with respect to these two cases. In the former, even assuming certainty and full information, underperception is found to depend mainly upon the fact that the object of perception is the "net tax liability", defined as the present value of future tax liability, net of the greater convenience derived in the present from financial investment in government bonds, compared

113

with other forms of financial investment. In the latter case, it is the difference between contributions and benefits which is the object of perception, i.e. the "net social security liability". A systematic underestimation of such a liability is likely to arise as a consequence of the ageing of population. The implication is that the demand for pension provisions might evolve without fully taking into account the liability involved. On the other hand, the financial impact of the ageing of population on the fulfilment of PAYG obligations deserves to be taken into account. In fact, in the presence of ageing, even to keep a constant replacement rate, implies a rising pension burden on working generations. The consideration of such a phenomenon, which can be thought of as a particular application of the well known Baumol's Law, stresses the uncertainty of pension fulfilment because of the unfunded nature of this implicit debt. This model leaves room for investigating whether inter-generational conflicts are likely to arise and how the likelihood of their occurrence can be reduced by devising alternative forms of fulfilment. More precisely, this latter point of view seems to suggest that methods of fulfilment which imply a "fair sharing" of demographic risk between generations are called for. These methods, in fact, would reduce the uncertainty related to the fulfilment of unfunded obligations and, therefore, would "stabilise" the contract.

8.3 Indeed, the occurrence of inter-generational conflicts very much depends on the hypotheses regarding the functioning of the collective decision-making process involved and on the behavioural assumptions with respect to the participants in such a process.

To transform individual decisions into political outcomes a stylised model of the functioning of collective decision-making is required. A demand-oriented model seems to fit with the redistributive nature of the pension issue and the application of the median voter theorem to the pension case is worth considering. Nor do the difficulties usually outlined in applying the median voter approach seem to prevent the application of the theorem in the pension case. The median voter can be identified in the median aged individual and his identity changes according to demographic changes. In the presence of ageing trends, the pivotal voter becomes older and more positively inclined toward pension provisions. Such a preference, however, is likely to find a constraint in the above mentioned awareness of the uncertainty of the obligation and in the risk of having his entitlements rejected in the future. A further constraint is to be found in the fact that increasing contribution rates may discourage work effort and, therefore, reduce the amount of resources available for inter-generational redistribution. Analytically, it follows that while a positive relationship is found to exist between median age and the optimal contribution rate when the impact of the contribution rate is ignored, such a relationship does not necessarily hold, and becomes ambiguous, when this impact is explicitly introduced into the analysis. Therefore, the demand for pension cannot be said to increase continuously when the median voter becomes older, at least as long as the

PAYG budget is balanced. This argument should be contrasted with the results reached in the public choice literature and claiming that pension systems, though burdensome for working generations, are likely to be perpetuated as long as it is in the majority's interest. As a result, a less pessimistic view of future developments of the PAYG system should be taken into account and the arguments for abolishing it seem to become weaker.

8.4 The outcome of the political process becomes more difficult to predict when the existence of interest groups is allowed for. The simple demand-oriented model "one man one vote" underlying the median voter approach is not able to capture all the features of political participation because different votes may have different weights. The extent of such a phenomenon in the social security case depends on the features of the social security system and, more precisely, on whether there exist many different potential interests, as represented by various social security schemes. Other things being equal, namely the age structure of the population, a larger number of pressure groups would imply a greater demand for pension provisions. In this demand for intra-generational redistribution age does not necessarily play a relevant role. On the other hand, in a rather homogeneous system, where only the inter-generational redistribution matters, not only is age influential but also the intensity of political participation. In fact, ageing, implying an increasing social security burden on the working generation, is likely to stimulate workers to influence the political decision-making outcome. The impact of ageing, therefore, might be partially counterbalanced by the impact of such participation and, as a result, the outcome of the political process cannot be unambiguously predicted and becomes a matter of empirical investigation.

Interesting insights rather than clear-cut conclusions can be derived from the empirical analysis. The relevant differences arising between cross-section and time-series results would suggest that a close link does exist between pension systems and socio-economic and political features characterising each country. At the same time, this consideration would provide some support for dealing with the pension issue within a public choice approach, which is sophisticated enough to grasp the complexity of the evolution of the pension system. The demand-oriented approach developed in this study seems to be confirmed by the regression results, at least as far as the median voter hypothesis is concerned. Other hypotheses which complement the median voter hypothesis, such as the fiscal illusion and the voluntary redistribution approaches, have been tested for. They turn out not to be fully satisfactory, probably because of the indicators used. On the other hand, available data did not allow for constructing other indicators. The testing for the pressure groups hypothesis suffers the same limitation. However, the results achieved so far would suggest that the demand-oriented model outlined above shows an encouraging explanatory power as far as the evolution of pension systems is concerned and is therefore worth exploring further.

Bibliography

AA.VV. (1983), *Ricostruzione della popolazione residente per sesso, età e regione*, Università degli studi "la Sapienza", Dipartimento di Scienze demografiche, Roma.

Aaron, A. (1966), The Social Insurance Paradox, in *Canadian Journal of Economics*, vol. 32, n. 3, pp. 371–374.

Aaron, A. (1982), *Economic Effects of Social Security*, Brooking Institutions, Washington D.C.

Akerloff, G.A. (1980), A Theory of Social Custom, of Which Unemployment May Be One Consequence, in *The Quarterly Journal of Economics*, vol. 94, n. 2, pp. 749–775.

Akerloff, G.A. (1984), *An Economic Theorist's Book of Tales*, Cambridge University Press.

Artoni, R. (1987), La riforma del sistema pensionistico, in *Politica economica*, n. 1, pp. 3–15.

Atkinson, A and J.E. Stiglitz (1980), *Lectures on Public Economics*, McGraw Hill.

Barro, R. (1974), Are Government Bonds Net Wealth?, in *Journal of Political Economy*, vol. 82, n. 6, pp. 1095–1118.

Barro, R. (1989), The Ricardian Approach to Budget Deficits, in *The Journal of Economic Perspectives*, vol. 3, n. 2, pp. 37–54.

Baumol, W. (1967), Macroeconomics of Unbalanced Growth: the Anatomy of Urban Crisis, in *The American Economic Review*, vol. 57, n. 3, pp. 415–426.

Becker, G.S. (1983), A Theory of Competition among Pressure Groups for Political Influence, in *The Quarterly Journal of Economics*, vol. 98, n. 3, pp. 371–400.

Becker, G.S. (1986), The Public Interest Hypothesis Revisited: A New Test of Peltzman's Theory of Regulation, in *Public Choice*, vol. 49, n. 2, pp. 223–234.

Becker, G. and K. Murphy (1988), The Family and the State, in *The Journal of Law and Economics*, vol. XXXI, n. 1, pp. 1–18.

Bennett, S.T. and T.J. Di Lorenzo (1984), Off-Budget Spending and the Economics of Local Government: Is the Median Voter Model Applicable?, in *Economia delle scelte pubbliche*, vol. 2, n. 2, pp. 85–96.

Bernheim, B.D. (1987), The Economic Effects of Social Security: Toward a Reconciliation of Theory and Measurement, in *Journal of Public Economics*, vol. 33, n. 3, pp. 273–304

118

Black, D. (1948), On the Rational of Group Decision-Making, in *Journal of Political Economy*, pp. 23–34.

Bollino, A. and N. Rossi (1988) Public Debt and Household's Demand for Monetary Assets in Italy, in F. Giavazzi and L. Spaventa (eds.), *High Public Debt: the Italian Experience,* Cambridge University Press, Cambridge, pp. 222–243.

Borgatta, E.F. and N.G. McCluskey (1980), *Aging and Society; Current Research and Policy Perspective,* Sage Publications.

Boskin, M. (1977a), Social Security and Retirement Decisions, in *Economic Inquiry,* vol. 15, n. 1, pp. 1–25.

Boskin, M. (1977b), Social Security: The Alternatives before Us, in M. Boskin (ed.), *The Crisis in Social Security: Problems and Prospects,* Institute for Contemporary Studies, San Francisco, pp. 173–186.

Boskin, M. (1982), Federal Government Deficits: Some Myths and Realities, in *The American Economic Review,* vol. 72, n. 2, Papers and Proceedings, pp. 296–303.

Boskin, M. (1986), *Too Many Promises: the Uncertain Future of Social Security,* Dow Jones Irwin, Homewood, Illinois.

Boskin, M. (1987), *Concepts and Measures of Federal Deficits and Debt and Their Impact on Economic Activity,* NBR Working Papers, n. 2332.

Boskin, M. and L. Kotlikoff (1985), *Public Debt and U.S. Saving: a New Test of the Neutrality Hypothesis,* Carnegie-Rockester Conference Series.

Breyer, F., J.M. Graf and D. Schulenburg (1987), Voting on Social Security: the Family as the Decision-Making Unit, in *Kyklos,* vol. 40, n. 4, pp. 529–547.

Brown, C.V. (1983), *Taxation and Incentive to Work,* Oxford University Press, Oxford.

Brown, C.V. and P.M. Jackson (1986), *Public Sector Economics,* III ed. Blackwell, Oxford.

Browne-Katz, W.P. and L. Olson (1983), *Aging and Public Policy. The Politics of Growing Old in America,* Greenwood Press.

Browning, E.K. (1973), Social Insurance and Intergenerational Transfers, in *Journal of Law and Economics,* vol. 16, n. 2, pp. 215–237.

Browning, E.K. (1975), Why the Social Insurance Budget is too Large in a Democracy, in *Economic Inquiry,* vol. 13, n. 3, pp. 373–388.

Browning, E.K. (1985), The Marginal Social Security Tax on Labor, in *Public Finance Quarterly,* vol. 13, n. 3, pp. 227–252.

Buchanan, J. (1958),*Public Principles of Public Debt,* Irwin, Homewood.

Buchanan, J. (1964a), *Public Finance in Democratic Process,* Chapel Hill, North Carolina Press.

Buchanan, J. (1964b), Public Debt, Cost Theory and the Fiscal Illusion, in J.M. Ferguson (ed.), *Public Debt and Future Generations,* The University of North-Carolina Press, Chapel Hill, pp. 150–162.

Buchanan, J. (1968), Social Insurance in a Growing Economy: A Proposal for Radical Reform, in *National Tax Journal,* vol. 21, n. 4, pp. 386–395.

Buchanan, J. (1976), Barro on the Ricardian Equivalence Theorem, in *Journal of Political Economy,* vol. 84, n. 2, pp. 337–342.

Buchanan, J. (1983), Social Security Survival: A Public Choice Perspective, in *The Cato Journal,* vol. 3, n. 2, pp. 339–353.

Buchanan, J., C. Rowley and R. Tollison (1987), *Deficits,* Blackwell, Oxford.

Buchanan, J. and R. Wagner(1977), *Democracy in Deficit: the Political Legacy of Lord Keynes,* Academic Press, London.

Buiter, W. and J. Tobin (1979), Debt Neutrality: A Brief Review of Doctrine and Evidence, in G. von Furstenberg (ed.), *Social Security versus Private Saving,* Ballinger, Cambridge, Mass., pp. 39–64.

Burkhauser, R.V. and J.A. Turner (1985), Is the Social Security Payroll Tax a Tax?, in *Public Finance Quarterly,* vol. 13, n. 3, pp. 253–268.

Burtless, G. and R. Moffitt (1984), Effects of Social Security Benefits on Labour Supply, in H. Aaron and G. Burtless (eds.), *Retirement and Economic Behaviour,* The Brookings Institution, Washington D.C., pp. 135–174.

Byatt, I. (1986), Public Debt in the U.K.: Trends, Composition and Economic Performance, in B.P. Herber (ed.), *Public Finance and Public Debt,* Wayne State University Press, Detroit, pp. 97–110.

Carter, R. (1982), Beliefs and Errors in Voting Choices: A Restatement of the Theory of Fiscal Illusion, in *Public Choice,* vol. 39, n. 3, pp. 343–360.

Castellino, O. (1981), La previdenza sociale in Italia: quanto sociale e quanto previdente?, in *Rivista di politica economica,* n. 2, pp. 135–170.

Castellino, O. (1984), Incertezze e insicurezze nell'attuale quadro della previdenza sociale, in *Economia pubblica,* n. 6, pp. 333–338.

Castellino, O. (1985), C'è un secondo debito pubblico (più grande del primo)?, in *Moneta e credito,* vol. 38, n. 149, pp. 21–30.

Castellino, O. (1987a), Debito pubblico e politica previdenziale. Il debito previdenziale, in F. Bruni (a cura di), *Debito pubblico e politica economica in Italia,* Collana Giorgio Rota, n. 1, SIPI, Roma, pp. 75–92.

Castellino, O. (1987b), Commento all'articolo di Artoni, in *Politica economica,* n. 1, pp. 17–22.

Cavaco Silva, A. (1977), *Economic Effects of Public Debt,* M. Robertson, Oxford.

CER (1987), *Previdenza pubblica e previdenza privata,* Roma, Rapporto n. 2.

Coale, J.A. (1972), *The Growth and Structure of Human Population. A Mathematical Investigation,* Princeton University Press, Princeton.

Craig, E.D. and A.J. Heins (1980), The Effect of Tax Elasticity on Government Spending, in *Public Choice,* vol. 35, n. 3, pp. 267–275.

Creedy, J. and R. Disney (1988), The New Pension Scheme in Britain, in *Fiscal Studies,* vol. 9, n. 2, pp. 57–71.

Culyer, A.J. (1980), *The Political Economy of Social Policy,* M.Robertson, Oxford.

De Viti De Marco, A. (1939), *Principi di economia finanziaria*, Einaudi, Torino, 1939, II ed.

Dilnot, A. and S. Webb (1988), The 1988 Social Security Reform, in *Fiscal Studies*, vol. 9, n. 3, pp. 26–53.

Eisner, R. (1984), Which Budget Deficit? Some Issues of Measurement and Their Implications, in *The American Economic Review*, vol. 74, n. 2, Papers and Proceedings, pp. 138–143.

Eisner, R. and P.J. Pieper (1984), A New View of the Federal Debt and Budget Deficits,in *The American Economic Review*, vol. 74, n. 1, pp. 11–29.

Eurostat (1977), *Social Accounts*, Luxembourg.

Eurostat (1982), *Caractéristiques Economiques et Sociales des Ménages dans la Communauté Européenne*, Luxembourg.

Feldstein, M. (1974), Social Security, Induced Retirement and Aggregate Capital Accumulation, in *Journal of Political Economy*, vol. 82, n. 5, pp. 905–926.

Feldstein, M. (1976a), Social Security and Saving: The Extended Life-Cycle Theory, in *The American Economic Review*, vol. 66, n. 2, Papers and Proceedings, pp. 77–86.

Feldstein, M. (1976b), Perceived Wealth in Bonds and Social Security: A Comment, in *Journal of Political Economy*, vol. 84, n. 2, pp. 331–336.

Feldstein, M. (1982), Government Deficits and Aggregate Demand, in *Journal of Monetary Economics*, vol. 9, n. 1, pp. 1–20.

Feldstein, M. (1985), Debt and Taxes in the Theory of Public Finance, in *Journal of Public Economics*, vol. 28, n. 2, pp. 233–245.

Ferguson, J.M. (1964), *Public Debt and Future Generations*, University of North Carolina Press, Chapel Hill.

Frey, B. (1978), *Modern Political Economy*, M.Robertson, Oxford.

Friedman, B.H. (1985), *Crowding out or Crowding in? Evidence on Debt Equity Substitutability*, NBER Working Papers n. 1565.

Friedman, M. (1953), Choice, Chance and the Personal Distribution of Income, in *Journal of Political Economy*, vol. 61, n. 4, pp. 277–290.

Gandenberger, O. (1986), On Government Borrowing and False Political Feedbacks, in B.P. Herber (ed.), *Public Finance and Public Debt*, Wayne State University Press, Detroit, pp. 205–216.

Giardina, E. (1965), Debito pubblico e teoria delle decisioni, in F. Forte and S. Lombardini (a cura di), *Saggi di economia*, Giuffrè, Milano, pp. 53–113.

Goldberg, V.P. (1980), Relational Exchange, in *American Behavioural Scientist*, vol. 23, n. 3, pp. 337–352.

Greene, K.V. (1986), The Public Choice of Differing Degrees of Tax Progressivity, in *Public Choice*, vol. 49, n. 3, pp. 265–282.

Halter, W.A. and R. Hemming (1987), The Impact of Demografic Change on Social Security Financing, in *IMF Staff Papers*, n. 3, pp. 471–502.

Hausman, J.A. (1985), Taxes and Labour Supply, in A.J. Auerbach and M.

Feldstein (eds.), *Handbook of Public Economics,* North-Holland, Amsterdam.

Heller, P., R. Hemming and P. Kohnert (1986), *Aging and Social Expenditure in the Major Industrialized Countries, 1980–2025,* IMF Occasional Paper n. 47.

Hemming, R. and J.A. Kay (1982), The Cost of the State Earning Related Pension Scheme, in *The Economic Journal,* vol. 92, n. 2, pp. 300–319.

Hills, J. (1984), What is the Public Sector Worth?, in *Fiscal Studies,* vol. 5, n. 1, pp. 19–35.

Holcombe, R.G. (1977), The Florida System: A Bowen Equilibrium Referendum Process, in *National Tax Journal,* vol. XXX, n. 1, pp. 77–84.

Holcombe, R.G., J.H. Jackson and H. Zardkoohi (1981), The National Debt Controversy, in *Kyklos,* vol. 34, n. 2, pp. 186–202.

INPS (1987), *Il futuro del sistema pensionistico italiano,* Roma.

ISTAT (A), *Annuario statistico,* Roma (various years).

ISTAT (B),*Popolazione, movimento anagrafico, famiglie e convivenze,* Roma (various years).

ISTAT (1981), *Bollettino mensile di statistica,* Supplemento n. 8, Roma.

ISTAT (1983), *Bollettino mensile di statistica,* Supplemento n. 28, Roma.

ISTAT (1985), *Bollettino mensile di statistica,* Supplemento n. 14, Roma.

ISTAT (1986), *Annuario di statistiche del lavoro,* Roma.

ISTAT (1987), *Annuario di contabilità nazionale,* vol. 1, Roma.

ISTAT (1988), *Statistiche della previdenza, della sanità e dell'assistenza sociale,* Roma.

Keyfitz, N. (1977), *Applied Mathematical Demography,* John Wiley & Sons, New York.

Kessler, D., S. Perelman and P. Pestieau (1986), Public Debt, Tax and Consumption: A Test on OECD Countries, in *Public Finance,* vol. 41, n. 1, pp. 63–70.

Kormendi, R.C. (1983), Government Debt, Government Spending and Private Sector Behaviour, in *The American Economic Review,* vol. 73, n. 5, pp. 994–1010.

Koskela, E. and M. Viren (1983),National Debt Neutrality: Some International Evidence, in *Kyklos,* vol. 36, n. 4, pp. 575–588.

Kotlikoff, L.J. (1987), Justifying Public Provision of Social Security, in *Journal of Policy Analysis and Management,* n. 4, pp. 674–689.

Leibenstein, H. (1976), *Beyond Economic Man: A New Foundation for Microeconomics,* Cambridge, Harvard University Press.

Lynn, R.J. (1983), *The Pension Crisis,* Lexington, Mass.

Marenzi, A. (1987), La teoria delle scelte collettive: il teorema dell'elettore mediano e le verifiche econometriche, in *Rivista di diritto finanziario e scienza delle finanze,* n. 1, pp. 151–167.

Maser, S.M. (1985), Demographic Factors Affecting Constitutional Decisions, in *Public Choice,* vol. 47, n. 1, pp. 121–162.

Meltzer, A.H. and S.F. Richard (1981), A Rational Theory of the Size of Government, in *Journal of Political Economy*, vol. 89, pp. 914–927.

Ministero del Tesoro (1986), *La spesa pubblica in Italia*, Roma.

Modigliani, F. and T. Jappelli (1987), Fiscal Policy and Saving in Italy since 1960, in M. Boskin, J.S. Fleming and S. Gorini (eds.), *Private Saving and Public Debt*, Blackwell, Oxford, pp. 126–170.

Modigliani, F., T. Jappelli and M. Pagano (1985), L'impatto della politica fiscale e dell'inflazione sul risparmio nazionale: il caso italiano,in *Moneta e credito*, 1985, n. 150, pp. 123–162.

Morcaldo, G. (1987), Commento all'articolo di Artoni, in *Politica economica*, n. 1, pp. 23–28.

Mueller, D. (1979), *Public Choice*, Cambridge University Press.

Mueller, D.C. and P. Murrell (1985), Interest Groups and the Political Economy of Government Size, in A. Peacock and F. Forte (eds.), *Public Expenditure and Government Growth*, Blackwell, Oxford, pp. 13–36.

Mueller, D.C. and P. Murrell (1986), Interest Groups and the Size of Government,in *Public Choice*, vol. 48, n. 2, pp. 125–146.

Munnel, A. (1974), *The Effects of Social Security on Personal Saving*, Ballinger, Cambridge.

Murrell, P. (1984), An Examination of the Factors Affecting the Formation of Interest Groups in OECD Countries, in *Public Choice*, vol. 43, n. 2, pp. 151–171.

Musgrave, R.A. (1981), A Reappraisal of Financing Social Security, in F. Skidmore (ed.), *Social Security Financing*, The MIT Press, Cambridge, pp. 89–127.

Niskanen, W.A. (1978), Deficits, Government Spending and Inflation, in *Journal of Monetary Economics*, vol. 4, n. 4, pp. 591–602.

OECD (1976), *Public Expenditure on Income Maintenance Programmes*, Paris.

OECD (1985), *Dépenses Sociales, 1960–1990. Problèmes de Croissance et de Maitrise*, Paris.

OECD (1987), *National Accounts (1974–1983)*, Paris.

OECD (1988a), *Labour Force Statistics, 1963–1983*, Paris.

OECD (1988b), *Revenue Statistics, 1965–1984*, Paris.

OECD (1988c), *Ageing Populations. The Social Policy Implications*, Paris.

OECD (1988d), *Reforming Public Pensions*, Social Policy Studies n. 5, Paris.

Olson, M. (1965), *The Logic of Collective Action*, Harvard University Press, Cambridge, Mass.

Onofri, P. (1988), Analisi empirica delle relazioni tra consumo e debito pubblico in Italia (1970–1984), in A. Graziani (a cura di), *La spirale del debito pubblico*, Il Mulino, Bologna, pp. 77–89.

Panella, G. (1982),*I trasferimenti di reddito a fini sociali: struttura ed evoluzione della spesa per pensioni*, Econpubblica, Milano.

Pareto, V. (1917), Lettere a Benvenuto Griziotti, in *Rivista di diritto finanziario e scienza delle finanze*, 1948, n. 2, pp. 133–140.

123

D.O. Parsons and D.R. Munro (1977), Inter-generational Transfers in Social Security, in M. Boskin (ed.), *The Crisis in Social Security: Problems and Prospects,* Institute for Contemporary Studies, San Francisco, pp. 65–86.

Peacock, A. (1979), *The Economic Analysis of Government and Related Themes,* M.Robertson, Oxford.

Peacock, A. (1986), Is There a Public Debt "Problem" in Developed Countries?, in B.P. Herber (ed.) Public Finance and Public Debt, Wayne State University Press, Detroit, pp. 29–42.

Peacock, A.T. and I. Rizzo (1987), Government Debt and the Growth in Public Spending, in *Public Finance,* n. 2, pp. 283–291.

Peltzman, S. (1976), Toward a More General Theory of Regulation, in *Journal of Law and Economics,* vol. 19, n. 2, pp. 211–240.

Pommerehne, W. (1980), Public Choice Approaches to Explain Fiscal Redistribution, in K.W. Roskamp (ed.), *Public Choice and Public Finance,* Cujas, Paris, pp. 169–190.

Pommerehne, W. and F. Schneider (1978), Fiscal Illusion, Political Institutions and Local Public Spending, in *Kyklos,* vol. 31, n. 3, pp. 381–408.

Puviani, A. (1903), *Teoria dell' illusione finanziaria,* Palermo.

Rizzo, I. (1985), Note intorno alla definizione del concetto di debito pubblico,in *Rivista italiana di diritto finanziario e scienza delle finanze,* n. 2, pp. 185–204.

Rizzo, I. (1988), *Fiscal Perception and Public Debt: Some Notes on the Equivalence Issue,* in Economia delle scelte pubbliche, n. 3, pp. 213–226.

Rizzo, I. (1989), *The Fulfilment of Unfunded Obligations and Baumol's Law,* in *Rivista di diritto finanziario e scienza delle finanze,* 1989, n. 3, pp. 404–418.

Rix, S. and P. Fisher (1982), *Retirement Age Policy: An International Perspective,* Pergamon Press, New York.

Rodgers, J. (1974), Explaining Income Redistribution,in H. Hochman and G. Peterson (eds.), *Redistribution through Public Choice,* Columbia University Press, New York, pp. 165–205.

Romer, T. (1975), Individual Welfare, Majority Voting and the Properties of a Linear Income Tax, in *Journal of Public Economics,* vol. 4, n. 2, pp. 163–185.

Romer, T. and H. Rosenthal (1979a), Bureaucrats versus Voters: On the Political Economy of Resource Allocation by Direct Democracy, in *The Quarterly Journal of Economics,* vol. 93, n. 4, pp. 563–587.

Romer, T. and H. Rosenthal (1979b), The Elusive Median Voter, in *Journal of Public Economics,* vol. 12, pp. 143–170.

Salysbury, R.H. (1975), Interest Groups, in F. Greenstein and N. Polsby (eds.), *Non-governmental Politics,* Reading, Mass.

Sen, A. (1987), *On Ethics and Economics,* Blackwell, Oxford.

Shaw, G.K. (1987), Macroeconomic Implications of Fiscal Deficits: an Expository Note, *Scottish Journal of Political Economy,* vol. 34, n. 2, pp. 192–198.

Shibata, H. and Y. Kimura (1986), Are Budget Deficits the Cause of Growth in

Government Expenditures?, in B.P. Herber (ed.), *Public Finance and Public Debt,* Wayne State University Press, Detroit, pp. 229–242.

Simon, H. (1955), A Behavioral Model of Rational Choice, in *The Quarterly Journal of Economics,* vol. 69, n. 1, pp. 99–118.

Simon, H. (1959), Theories of Decision Making in Economics and Behavioral Science, in *The American Economic Review,* vol. 49, n. 1, pp. 253–283.

Simon, H. (1972), Theories of Bounded Rationality, in C.B. Radner and R. Radner (eds.), *Decision and Organization,* North-Holland Publishing Company, Amsterdam, pp. 161–176.

Simon, H. (1976), From Substantive to Procedural Rationality, in Latsis, S. (ed.), *Method and Appraisal in Economics,* Cambridge University Press, pp. 129–148.

Spaventa, L. (1984), The Growth of Public Debt in Italy: Past Experience, Perspectives and Policy Problems, in *Banca Nazionale del Lavoro Quarterly Review,* n. 2, pp. 119–150.

Spaventa, L. (1988), Debito pubblico e pressione fiscale, in *Moneta e credito,* vol. XLI, n. 161, pp. 3–20.

Stearns, P.N. (1981), Political Perspective on Social Security Financing, in F. Skidmore (ed.), *Social Security Financing,* The MIT Press, Cambridge, pp. 173–223.

Stein, B. (1980), *Social Security and Pensions in Transition,* The Free Press, New York.

Stigler, G.J. (1971), The Theory of Economic Regulation, in *Bell Journal of Economics and Management Science,* vol. 2, n. 1, pp. 3–21.

Stiglitz, J.E. (1986), *Economics of the Public Sector,* W.W.Norton & Company, New York.

Tamburi, G. (1983), Escalation of State Pension Costs: The Reasons and the Issues, in *International Labour Review,* vol. 122, n. 3, pp. 313–327.

Thompson, L.M. (1983), The Social Security Reform Debate, in *Journal of Economic Literature,* vol. 21, n. 4, pp. 1425–1467.

Tullock, G. (1971), The Charity of the Uncharitable, in *Western Economic Journal,* vol. 9, pp. 379–392.

Tullock, G. (1984), *Economics of Income Redistribution,* Kluwer-Nijhoff, The Hague.

United Nations (1982), *Demographic Yearbook,* New York.

United Nations (1985a), *Statistical Yearbook,* New York.

United Nations (1985b), *World Population Prospects. Estimates and Projections as Assessed in 1982,* New York.

Verbon, H.A.A. (1986), Altruism, Political Power and Public Pension, in *Kyklos,* vol. 39, n. 3, pp. 343–358.

Weaver, C. (1982), *The Crisis in Social Security,* Duke Press, Durham.

Williamson, O.E. (1979), Transaction-Cost Economics: The Governance of Contractual Relations, in *Journal of Law and Economics,* vol. 22, n. 2, pp.

233–261.

Williamson, O.E. (1981), Contract Analysis: The Transaction Cost Approach, in P. Burrows and C.G. Veljanowsky (eds.), *The Economic Approach to Law,* Butterworths, London, pp. 39–60.

Yung-Ping Cheng (1982), Marrying, Divorcing, Living Together and Working: Effects of Changing American Family Structure on the Popularity of Social Security, in S.J. Bahr (ed.), *Economics and the Family,* Lexington Books, Lexington, pp. 150–173.

Index

128

and funded public debt, 22–23, 25
and irrational behaviour, 24–25
and median voter, 22, 61
and social security contributions, 37, 99
sources of, 39
Frey B., 18
Friedman B.H., 31, 42
Friedman M., 96
Future generations
protection of, 12

Gandenberger O., 18, 43
Giardina E., 25
Goldberg V.P., 19
Government
and interest groups, 83–84, 97
and need for political reputation, 11
measurement of the size of, 15
NTL perception and the size of, 15
and unfunded obligations fulfilment,
10–12, 50
Graf J.M., 109
Greene K.V., 109

Halter W.A., 19
Hausman J.A., 79
Heins A.J., 39
Heller P., 108
Hemming R., 19, 108
Hills J., 17, 19
Holcombe R.G., 40, 76

Imperfect information
and the perception of public debt, 27
Inps, 19
Interest groups
and economic regulation, 82
and fiscal rents, 83
and free-riding, 82, 90
and government size, 83–84, 97
and inter-generational redistribution,
86–87, 88, 107
and intra-generational redistribution,
87, 88, 106
and the demand for pensions, 85–88,
97–98, 101
and the political process, 81–85
factors underlying the formation of, 89
Isolation paradox, 10, 16, 32
Istat, 100, 111

Jackson J.H., 40
Jackson P.M., 77
Jappelli T., 40

Kay J.A., 19
Keyfitz N., 78
Kessler D., 40
Kimura Y., 40
Kohnert P., 108
Kormendi R.C., 40
Koskela E., 40
Kotlikoff L.J., 19, 40

Labour supply
elasticity of, 72, 76, 79
Leibenstein H., 53
Linear income tax, 58, 60
Life expectancy, 95, 109
Lynn R.J., 19

Marenzi A., 76
McCluskey N.G., 90
Median voter
and efficiency, 76
and fiscal illusion, 22, 61
and inter-generational redistribution, 59
and intra-generational redistribution,
57–59
and the political process, 55–56
and unfunded obligations, 63–72, 91
and population growth, 66
identification of, 55–57, 76
single peaked preferences, 56, 58–59,
61–62, 77
Meltzer A.H., 90
Ministero del Tesoro, 19
Modigliani F., 40
Moffitt R., 18
Morcaldo G., 19
Mueller D., 58, 83, 97
Munnel A., 18
Munro D.R., 12
Murphy K., 18
Murrell P., 83, 97, 110
Musgrave R.A., 12, 49, 53

Niskanen W.A., 23, 40

Oecd, 53, 93, 94, 109, 111
Olson L., 90
Olson M., 89
Onofri P., 41
Optimal tax theory, 58, 73

Pagano M., 40
Panella G., 111
Pareto V., 41
Parsons D.O., 12
PAYG system *see also* Unfunded

130

Substitution effects,
  between pensions and present wages,
  47–48, 65, 67

Tamburi G., 19
Thompson L.M., 18
Tobin J., 40
Tollison R., 17
Tullock G., 58, 72, 77, 91
Turner J.A., 110

Unfunded obligations
  analogies with explicit public debt, 5–6
  and intra-generational redistribution, 10
  and relational contracts, 7
  and risk sharing, 12, 49–50
  and saving, 13, 17
  and uncertainty, 9, 63

differences with explicit public debt,
  7–13
fulfilment of, 10–12, 43–49, 60, 63–72
United Nations, 93, 109

Verbon H.A.A., 53
Viren M., 40

Wealth effects, 47–48, 65
Weaver C., 19
Wagner R., 19, 22
Webb S., 14
Williamson O.E., 7, 18

Yung-Ping Cheng, 109

Zardkoohi H., 40

FINANCIAL AND MONETARY POLICY STUDIES

FINANCIAL AND MONETARY POLICY STUDIES

19. I. Rizzo: *The 'Hidden' Debt.* With a Foreword by A.T. Peacock. 1990
ISBN 0-7923-0610-4
* 20. D.E. Fair and C. de Boissieu (eds.): *Financial Institutions in Europe under New Competitive Conditions.* 1990
ISBN 0-7923-0673-2

*Published on behalf of the *Société Universitaire Européenne de Recherches Financières* (SUERF), consisting the lectures given at Colloquia, organized and directed by SUERF.

Further information about *Economy* publications are available on request.

Kluwer Academic Publishers – Dordrecht / Boston / London

DATE DUE

~~DEC 2 3 2000~~			
~~MAR 1 1 2001~~			
JUL 1 2 2001			
			Printed in USA

HIGHSMITH #45230